lifehacked

HOW ONE FAMILY FROM THE SLUMS
MADE **MILLIONS** FROM SELLING APPS

ALLEN WONG

ISBN: 1480178918
ISBN-13: 978-1480178915

To everyone who supported my family.

CONTENTS

PREFACE

What you are about to read is a detailed story about the experiences my parents and I faced while dealing with the unfortunate circumstances that we were given. All of the lessons I learned from those experiences are weaved into the story along with an explanation as to how they molded me. The story wraps up with how I used that knowledge to create and market some of the best-selling apps available in the App Store®. Overall, it's a philosophical and anecdotal guide to life that takes you through the major events in my life as well as my parents' lives.

Before we begin, here are a few things that you should know prior to reading this book:

Lifehacks

The term 'life hack' (or 'lifehack') used to refer to tricks that computer programmers used for increasing productivity by cutting through the information overload and organizing their data. It has since been expanded to describe any trick, skill, shortcut, or clever method to increase productivity and efficiency in any part of your life. For the purpose of this book, the term 'lifehack' will be defined as any life lesson that brings you closer to reaching your goals in life.

Most of you are more familiar with the phrase 'thinking outside of the box'. Learning to solve problems in a clever and unorthodox way is just one of the many methods for getting ahead in life. And learning how to think outside of the box has been one of those pivotal life lessons (or lifehacks) that changed the way I solved problems, the way I socialized, and the way I viewed the world.

I picked up many of these important lifehacks on my decades-long journey to the top. Some were passed down from generations upon generations of my family. Some were picked up by observing and learning from the successful people around me. And some were created by me through discovery, creativity and experimentation.

Origin of the Book

While I was growing up, I noticed that several parents were struggling at raising their children. Even though the proper way of raising a child can be highly subjective, I have the luxury of hindsight and can compare my peers' current standings with how they were raised when they were younger. Sometimes parents are not to be blamed for their bad parenting skills. Some parents were taught parenting skills by people who did not understand children so well. While I believe that their intentions are good, I also believe that some people just forget what it is like to be a child after a few decades. Or they never possessed the knowledge on how to raise their children to begin with.

As a teenager, this made me wonder if I would grow up to be one of those parents who did not understand their children and did not raise them properly. So instead of risking it and winging it in the future, I kept a journal with most of the parenting tips and lifehacks that I picked up along the way. I had been updating this journal for over a decade now, and it was originally intended either to remind me of what I learned or to teach my future children all of the important things I learned. The latter reason was meant for a situation where I pass away before I get a chance to teach them the lessons first-hand.

After I did an interview with Secret Entourage® and told a much shortened version of my success story, I noticed that there was a growing demand for more about my life and what I learned through the obstacles that I faced. That was when I figured that instead of keeping all of these lifehacks to myself and my family, I could share them and help others improve their quality of life and succeed.

So what you are about to read is a compilation of lifehacks that took me years to complete. It is written and organized in a comprehensive manner that takes you through the decades of my life as well as the lives of the people around me. Those who read my Secret Entourage interview know that I have been through many years of pain and stressful torment. But with each obstacle, I adapted quickly and learned to survive better.

Becoming Lifehacked

The term 'hacker' has been given a negative connotation by various news outlets. Thus, people have associated hackers with the cybercrimes that are committed by criminals with the intent to do harm. What most people do not know is that the word 'hacker' can have a completely different meaning from this. A hacker to me is someone who challenges the existing order. Thus, a person who is lifehacked is someone who does not accept a predetermined place in society. A person who is lifehacked is someone who does not do things strictly the old-fashioned way. A person who is lifehacked is someone who stares down a seemingly impassible roadblock in life and finds over a dozen different ways to circumvent it.

So, if you are looking for a book to tell you exactly what to do in your life, then this is not the book for you. This book instead teaches you how to think rather than what to think. The key challenge to being successful is learning how to be an independent individual rather than a person who depends on others for guidance or money.

Millionaire from the Slums

There is a story behind each lifehack I picked up. By taking you through my past, you will pick up on these lifehacks as well and hopefully become a better person by learning from them. Because of this, those who read this book tend to draw comparisons with the 2008 movie, *Slumdog Millionaire*. Like Jamal, the protagonist in the movie, I, too, have been through a rough life before becoming a millionaire. I, too, came from a family that grew up in the slums of Asia. And like Jamal, I, too, never gave up on life and the pursuit of happiness. The difference is that Jamal used the knowledge he gained from his unfortunate childhood to win money on a TV quiz show, while I used the knowledge I learned from my unfortunate life to create multimillion-dollar businesses.

Spoiler alert: In the end of that movie, it was determined that Jamal succeeded because "it was written" (meaning that he was destined to win). However, believing that your fate has already been predetermined is detrimental to succeeding.

Always believe that you can turn your luck around at any moment, because each new day could be the start of a new you. Most successful businesses were built from the ground up. So, do not stop trying to be successful in life unless you are completely satisfied with what you currently have. As Steve Jobs, co-founder of Apple®, once advised, "Stay Hungry. Stay Foolish."

You, too, can hack your life. Just by having the right mindset, you are already setting in motion your vehicle to a better life.

By choosing to hack your life, you are pledging to let no tough situations in life defeat you. You may lose some battles here and there, but you are determined to win the war. I made this pledge over a decade ago, when the circumstances were against me. By the time you finish this book, you will have the necessary tools and knowledge to make the same pledge and to push aside the things that are hindering you from reaching your full potential.

This is my journey. These are my battles. This is my life... hacked.

1 SKYROCKET

It was morning in New York City, but I was still awake from the night before. Sleepless nights were fast becoming the norm. For most people, chirping birds and sunrises were nature's morning calls. For me, they were pats on the back for another productive night. I had just made an update on my flagship app, "5-0 Radio". I was trying a new marketing technique, and was waiting eagerly for the results.

At this point, I had been coding apps for about a year, but this was still considered early in my career. I was still working at a nine-to-five job. I was still living in my mother's basement. I was still addicted to the rush of making limitless money. While staring at the screen in the dark basement, I kept refreshing the App Store rank charts and kept pressing "F5" on my keyboard like an anxious druggie waiting for his next fix.

Watching my apps climb the charts was probably the best part of the job. Even though it has no effect on its sales, watching my app do well in the market to this day still gives me immense pleasure.

1

"You reap what you sow," as they say. And I sowed something big this time. I was just not prepared for how big this would become.

As I was watching the rankings, I noticed that there was something strange about the way my app was moving up the charts. Normally, my apps would raise maybe five positions every hour after a new release or a new update. But this time, things were different. It jumped ten positions in just fifteen minutes. I thought that it was just a glitch. So, I refreshed my browser again. It jumped ten more positions. I refreshed it again a few minutes later, and it jumped another ten positions. It was still a weekday, so I went to my office job. By the time I arrived at my workplace, my app had jumped another 50 positions.

"Holy *sheeht*," I mouthed quietly in my office, "This app is skyrocketing!" In my mind, it sounded much louder.

At that point, I was not only breaking my personal records; I was shattering them. By night, my app had broken into the top 100 paid apps chart. This was the most coveted spot by all developers. Only 100 apps could be in this spot at any given time, so being here was a sign that your app had made it. It was a badge of honor that only a few developers out of the hundreds of thousands of app developers achieved. And I had just achieved it.

I took a well-deserved sleep that night while eagerly waiting to wake up the next morning. To an app developer, the only thing better than watching your app rocket through the charts was getting the actual download and revenue numbers the next morning.

The numbers were nothing short of astounding. More than fifty thousand people downloaded my app that day. But that was not the end of it. The next day, eighty thousand more people downloaded the app. The app later became one of the top 10 apps with close to a hundred thousand new users per day. I had come a long way since the days of making only fifty dollars a day. And when I took a step back to view the bigger picture, I realized that my entire family had come a long way since the days of being in the slums.

2 TIGER PARENTS

My life story begins with my parents. Those of you who read or heard of the 2011 book, *Battle Hymn of the Tiger Mother* by Amy Chua, would be familiar with the term 'Tiger Parenting'. For those who are unfamiliar, 'Tiger Parenting' is the practice of traditional, strict child-rearing with the goal of academic success while steering them towards certain career paths.

With that being said, my parents, while traditional in many other ways, were not tiger parents. They were never very strict when it came for me to choose what I wanted to do with my life. I got to where I am today, not because my parents forced me to do certain things. Instead, their parenting worked out well because they taught me great life lessons and led by example.

Some of you may not have had an advantageous upbringing. Perhaps your parents both worked and never paid attention to you. Perhaps they were too poor to afford to buy you things and put you in a private school. Perhaps they were too strict, and pushed you to become someone who you were not. You may choose to spend the rest of your life blaming your parents and others for not being successful. Or you may realize that all of that does not matter now. You are ultimately in control of what is going to happen to the rest of your life.

The Slums

Do not get stuck on the belief that only the rich get richer, or that because you do not have wealthy parents, then you will never be wealthy. According to *Millionaire Next Door* by Thomas J. Stanley, Ph.D. and William D. Danko, Ph.D., 80 percent of millionaires were first-generation millionaires. This meant that their parents' wealth was not the deciding factor that made them rich. My own parents were not wealthy at all.

In fact, my father grew up in the slums of Guangzhou, China. His mother had passed away when he was really young, and his father wasn't around to take care of him. Thus, he became homeless as a little kid along with his siblings. They had to beg for food in order to stay alive. As a teenager, he was forced to work on farmland by the Chinese communist regime, because his family was too poor to afford an education for him. Instead of being given a high school education, my father was given farm tools and 100 lb. bags of rice to carry over his shoulders. He received only a few cents a day for his labor, and was eating mostly rice as sustenance. Meat was rationed and scarce to him, so he was malnourished as a child. Thus, he only grew to the height of 5'3" despite having a father who was 5'9". By the time he was 18, he knew that he had to escape the communist regime in order to get a better life. At that time, Hong Kong was still controlled by the British government, so my father sought refuge there. However, the trip was not going to be an easy one.

The Great Escape

Not only was it illegal for my father to leave China for Hong Kong, it was also a perilous journey that required months of preparation and training. With several of his close friends, my father concocted a plan to cross the border that separated Hong Kong and China. At the border, he would have to swim over a long channel of water filled with oyster shells on the bottom and sharks prowling the surface. On top of that, there were coast guards who would search the waters for escapees and arrest or shoot those they caught.

The only other route of escape was to jump the barbed wire border fences that were patrolled by armed Chinese soldiers. Those soldiers were ordered to shoot and kill anyone attempting to escape. According to the 2010 book, *Big Fleeing* by Bingan Chen, there were so many refugees killed trying to escape this way that some people in Shenzhen even made a fortune from collecting the dead refugees. What had happened was that the Chinese government started a program that paid citizens 15 Yuan per body collected, because there were just too many dead refugees for them to handle alone.

Therefore, my father and his friends chose to swim across the channel instead. Their athletic build acquired from all of their farm labor helped them become avid swimmers. While this gave them a better chance at escape, they still planned their escape meticulously to better their chances at survival.

My father and his friends were all too familiar with the risks. They knew people who were caught, jailed, and beaten badly after failing to complete the same feat that they were about to do. But this was not going to deter them. They were brave, ambitious, and motivated to lead a life where the government would not keep oppressing them economically and physically.

This was actually my father's third attempt at crossing the channel. In the first two times, he was caught by coast guards and jailed for several months. They would torture him by withholding food from him, so that he would starve. They would try to use propaganda to convince him to stay in China. And they would interrogate him for hours to try to get him to tell them who helped him and who else was trying to escape.

So, he knew that this third attempt would be his last one. Going to jail for the third time for the same crime would carry much more extreme punishments. This was a do-or-die situation for him.

He was at the shore now with his friends. There was no turning back once they started swimming. This time around, he had a new route of entry to Hong Kong and new strategies to keep him and his friends from getting caught again.

When my father arrived at the channel, it was in the middle of the night. He looked at his friends and silently nodded to them. It was time. With nothing except for two tied-up plastic bags filled with old discarded tennis balls and a hollow bamboo stick, my dad and his friends began their long and dangerous swim to freedom.

To prevent themselves from cutting their feet on the oyster shells, they would have to swim without stopping for about an hour across the channel separating Shenzhen, China and the New Territories of Hong Kong. And they had to do all of this while fighting the currents that could wash them into the open ocean and while avoiding the sharks that prowled those waters.

While swimming through the treacherous waters in the dark, he and his friends would occasionally have to stay underwater to avoid being seen by the coast guards. Using the bamboo sticks, they were able to stay underwater for long periods of time. This, combined with the darkness of the night, caused them to lose sight of each other during the journey. That was the last time my father would see his friends again.

Once they reached the shore, they were on their own. My father would later find out that all of the friends he was with made it across safely. Hong Kong wasn't very populated at the time and welcomed all refugees. The government of Hong Kong saw Chinese refugees as sources of cheap labor and gave all of them citizenship.

The first thing my father did in Hong Kong was head to the nearest police station and register as a refugee hoping to gain citizenship to Hong Kong. Because my father never received a birth certificate, he actually never knew his real birthday. Since he arrived in Hong Kong on September 7th, 1966, he called September 7th, 1946 his birthday. He figured that he was starting a new life in Hong Kong anyway, so he might as well call that day his birthday.

After he got his papers, he rang up his older sister who was already in Hong Kong. She helped him find a place to live and a job as a Chinese herbalist. His older sister was also a refugee. Together, they thrived in Hong Kong, and my father became a great herbalist while reading herbalist books and studying under his boss. He eventually saved enough money from working to buy a plane ticket to the United States.

Lifehack #1: Be ambitious in the face of doubt.

These refugees were some of the bravest and most ambitious people in China. Their cheap labor and ambitions brought about Hong Kong's economic success in the late 20th century. Several of them even went on to becoming millionaires. Chen estimated in his book that 40 of the 100 richest men in Hong Kong were refugees from China.

This was no coincidence. One of the most important lifehacks that I had learned was to be ambitious even when doubt starts to flood your mind.

When I was younger, I used to be very afraid of roller coasters. The very first roller coaster that I had been on was Space Mountain, an indoor roller coaster that took place completely in the dark at

Disneyland. My cousin had brought me there when I was around 7.

Throughout the two-hour wait on the line, I was extremely nervous of riding it. I had an imaginative mind, so I thought of all the possible ways in which the ride could go wrong. My cousin, who was around my age, had no fears at all. I was baffled by his courage and felt inferior and embarrassed by my own cowardice. I wanted to go on the ride to show my bravery, but my body refused to cooperate.

When I finally got on the ride, my cousin was laughing and having blast, while I was clinging onto the handle bar as if it was my only friend in the world. But in the middle of the ride, things changed. My anxiety turned into excitement. When the ride was finally over, I no longer had a fear of roller coasters. I still got body chills and shaky nerves, but this time I embraced them. I didn't fight those sensations. I let those sensations intensify and I played with them. They made me feel alive.

Later in life, I would go on many other thrilling adventures, such as water-powered jetpacking, skydiving, and being shot up via a giant slingshot. I would have missed out on many thrilling adventures if I wasn't able to drown out the self-doubt and overcome my fears. You've probably been through a similar first-time roller coaster experience. Or perhaps you've once talked yourself out of asking someone out, because you let your self-doubt convince you that you were not good enough. And if you add your self-doubt to the doubt from your haters and peers, then you have a recipe for failure.

Curiosity may have killed the cat, but we're humans and not cats.

So be curious and ambitious, and take risks. You don't know how many things you are missing out on by fearing the unknown. As long as you plan accordingly to keep yourself afloat in case your ambitions fail, you will be fine. And even if your ambitions do fail, it is not truly a failure. You will learn from it and grow as a person.

Lifehack #2: Failure is not defeat.

There have been many people in history who were deemed as failures in the beginning. When rapper Eminem first rapped at a club, he was booed. He admitted years later that he almost quit rapping after that night because it was both extremely traumatizing and embarrassing. He was also a high school dropout who nearly died from overdosing on drugs. And he attempted suicide because he couldn't deal with the drug habit and poverty.

The Beatles were infamously rejected by Decca Records when they first auditioned for the record label. In regards to their rejection, the Decca Records explained, "Guitar groups are on the way out... the Beatles have no future in show business." They would later greatly regret that decision.

At a young age, Walt Disney was fired from his job at the Kansas City Star Newspaper company because his boss thought he lacked creativity. He later acquired his own animation studio called Laugh-O-Gram, where he hired a vast number of animators. However, the studio profits were not enough to cover the salaries paid to the employees and his studio went bankrupt. But that did not stop him.

He later started a studio in Hollywood, CA and the rest was history.

As you can see, failing is not necessarily the same as defeat. It is more of a delay to your eventual success. If you try to shoot a 3-pointer in basketball, you may fail the first few tries. But eventually, with enough practice, you will succeed.

True failure is never getting started in the first place.

"Don't fear failure. — Not failure, but low aim, is the crime. In great attempts, it is glorious even to fail."

– Bruce Lee

3 SOMETHING FROM NOTHING

With nothing but the shirt on his back, my father, in his late twenties, moved from Hong Kong to the United States in the 1970s. Back then, the United States was very welcoming of refugees and gave my father a green card after two years of living there. He eventually got citizenship after living there for seven years.

When he first moved to the U.S., my father was so poor that he resorted to sleeping at a YMCA. His living situation was basically a mattress among numerous other mattresses on the ground of a large dorm room. It was as close to homelessness as you could get without actually being homeless.

But despite his poverty, he still had dreams of obtaining a better life for himself and his future family. He figured that he could do so by putting his skills at administering herbal medicine to good use in the United States.

Since he was not formally educated on administering herbal medicine, he would spend whatever extra money he had earned on medical books. He owned shelves upon shelves of herbalist medical books. Eventually, he co-founded with his older brother an herbalist drugstore in New York City's Chinatown. That was also where he met my mother through a mutual friend and got married.

My mother also came from the slums. She and her family lived in the government projects in Hong Kong and had to borrow money to come to the United States in 1978. Since she also could not afford an education when she was younger and did not speak a lick of English, she was only able to get a job as a seamstress in a sweatshop in Chinatown.

After giving birth to my brother and me, my mother quit her job and became a homemaker for the rest her life. Even though she didn't bring income into the family, my mother still played a pivotal role in bringing our family out of poverty and into the upper class. She was the support that my father, brother, and I needed to get through each grueling day.

With the support from the entire family, the herbal pharmacy that my father co-founded went on to become one of the most popular herbalist/acupuncturist drugstores in New York City.

Lifehack #3: Realize that you can create wealth from nothing.

Some people doubt that they can become millionaires if they start with nothing. These doubters are either misinformed or simply making excuses for themselves for not trying harder. By doubting that they can become anything more than their peers can, they are doing themselves a disservice by not even taking a chance at success.

My father's story is proof that you can come from nothing and still make a decent living. And even during the great global recession of 2008, I was still able to make my first million dollars with only an investment of a hundred dollars or so. So, circumstance is not the deciding factor in your personal enrichment.

And there are many other success stories about people coming from poverty and making it. Eminem was raised in a trailer park. He is now a multimillionaire rapper, record producer, songwriter, and actor.

John Paul DeJoria had a pretty rough beginning as well. His parents divorced when he was two, and he sold Christmas cards and newspapers to support his family before he was even 10. He even became an L.A. gang member before he joined the military. He later took a $700 loan and created the John Paul Mitchell Systems. While living out of his car, he sold his company's shampoo door-to-door. His system now makes around $900 million annually.

Guy Laliberté used to eat fire and walk on stilts in the streets of Quebec. He later founded Cirque du Soleil and became a multi-billionaire.

Oprah Winfrey was living with her grandmother wearing dresses made out of potato sacks until the age of 6. She was later sexually assaulted by two members of her family and a family friend. That forced her to run away from home at age 13. When she was 14, she became pregnant and gave birth to her son, who died shortly afterwards. She later got a full scholarship to college, won a beauty pageant, and got discovered by a radio station. She later became the first female African-American billionaire.

According to his biography, Sam Walton used to live in a farm in Oklahoma during the Great Depression. He helped his family out by milking the cow and delivering the milk to the customers. He also sold magazine subscriptions and delivered newspapers. By the time he was 26, he was managing a variety store. He later took a loan from his father-in-law to buy a Ben Franklin variety store in Arkansas. He expanded his store into a chain, and later went on to create Wal-Mart and Sam's Club.

Ingvar Kamprad also lived in a farm growing up. While growing up in Sweden, he used to buy matches in bulk from Stockholm and sell them to his neighbors. He realized that he could start selling other things. So, he started selling fish, Christmas decorations, and pens. He later took money from his father to create a mail-order business. Furniture was his company's biggest seller, and he used local manufacturers to keep prices low. His company, IKEA, later became a multibillion dollar business. The name IKEA came from his initials along with the initials of his village and family farm.

Also from Europe, Leonardo Del Vecchio was given up by his widowed mother to an orphanage, because his mother could no longer support him. As an orphan, he worked in a factory, where he lost a piece of his index finger, making molds for auto parts and eyeglass frames. At 23, he opened his own molding shop that would later expand to the world's largest maker of sunglasses and prescription glasses. His company, Luxottica, is responsible for brands such as Ray-Ban, Persol, and Oakley, as well as 6,000 retail shops such as Sunglass Hut and LensCrafters. His company also makes sunglasses for designer brands such as Chanel, Prada, Burberry, Polo Ralph Lauren, Tiffany, Versace, Stella McCartney, Vogue, Miu Miu, Tory Burch and Donna Karan.

The list goes on and on for the people who start with nothing, but later become millionaires and billionaires. You truly can make enormous wealth from nothing. And for those who doubt that, history has something to say to them.

Lifehack #4: There are no limits; only plateaus.

If you start putting mental or physical limits on the things that you do, then it will show in your work and in your life. Athletes sometimes reach a point where they are not physically progressing further for a few weeks or even months. But, they haven't hit a physical limit yet. They've only hit a plateau. By changing up their routine and constantly pushing themselves, they can break through these plateaus.

That is why world records are constantly being broken. In 1945, the record for running a mile was held by a great Swedish athlete named Gunder Hägg at 4:01.4. For a long time, it was hard for people to imagine that anyone could run a mile in under four minutes. And that stood true for about a decade after Gunder's record mile run.

But then in 1954, the elusive four-minute mile was achieved by Roger Bannister in a mile run timed at 3:59.4. The four-minute mile has since then been achieved by many male athletes around world. Imagine if Roger held the belief that the four-minute mile could never be achieved. He would have stopped before the four-minute mile and given up.

But he kept on believing that he could do it. And he never gave up training until after he did it.

"Every morning in Africa, a gazelle wakes up. It knows it must outrun the fastest lion or it will be killed. Every morning in Africa, a lion wakes up. It knows it must run faster than the slowest gazelle, or it will starve. It doesn't matter whether you're a lion or a gazelle – when the sun comes up, you'd better be running." – Roger Bannister

This applies to life as well. If you continue to believe that you are limited by your circumstances or societal factors, then you will never break out of your plateaus. Instead of having psychological limitations and staying on the plateau, you should move beyond it.

The very first step to going beyond the plateau is to remove your fears. It is okay to be fearful of the unknown, because there is no hope without fear. But at the same time, there is no fear without hope. So rest assured that no matter how dire your situation may be and how fearful you are of the things to come, there is always hope and a chance to move forward.

It helps by knowing that there are others in similar or worse positions than you who have gone beyond their plateaus and achieved success. And it also helps by being around those who have experience with success.

Lifehack #5: Surround yourself with other successful people.

One of the other ways of staying in a hole and never achieving success is by surrounding yourself with doubters. And there will be many of these people on your way to the top.

These are the people who tell you that you should quit dreaming and should follow their own unsuccessful lives instead. These are the ones who are afraid of the unknown. They are only familiar with their own life, and have been spending so much time in it that they are satisfied with underachieving.

Often times, these are your closest friends or even your own parents. They mean well and aren't really trying to take you down. Instead, they have seen many failures in their lifetimes, and perhaps have failed in their own past. Therefore, they are simply trying to save you from the embarrassment, financial loss, and misery of failing at your business.

If you keep listening to the doubt, you might start believing it yourself. That is why you should surround yourself with people who are already successful and don't doubt that your success can be achieved.

And at the same time, be careful of those who are only interested in your money or mooching off of your success. They will cheer you on in the beginning and genuinely want to see you succeed. But when you do become successful, they will take credit for some of it and/or ask you to help them financially.

They will often say things along the lines of, "I helped you in the beginning, so now it's your turn to help me. Without me, you wouldn't have been successful. Don't forget the little people. Don't forget where you came from."

These yes-men start off as cheerleaders, but end up becoming nothing more than leeches. When people start taking credit for your success when they don't deserve the credit, then that is when it is time to part ways with them.

And on the flip-side, after you become successful, do not forget to thank and give back to the community that raised and molded you. You are not the only person in the universe trying to get through a tough life. Even if you feel that society never helped you reach your goals, you do have a moral obligation to give other people a fighting chance.

4 INVESTING WISELY

"A penny saved is a penny earned" – Benjamin Franklin

Despite making decent money as an herbalist, my father, who had borrowed money to start his store in Chinatown, continued to live frugally throughout his life. Our family focuses on value over extravagance. There is a Chinese proverb that goes, "Showing off your wealth is a fool's idea of glory." By saving and investing your money, you will end up wealthier in the long run. Wait until you have more money than you need to save before you start splurging.

Living Frugally

One of the things I admired about my father was his self-sacrifice. He could have bought a luxury sedan to get to work every day, but instead he rode a bike to work each morning. The whole commute took him maybe an extra hour or so of commuting each day. It was a tedious and time-consuming commute, but he did it to save money. Our whole family had followed suit.

Our family car was an old $15,000 family sedan which we kept in our family even to this day. Its fuel efficiency and low cost were what appealed to my family. Even though we had this family car, my father never drove it. The car was used sparingly by my mother to drive to places that we could not reach by foot or public transportation. My mother didn't even use the car to get groceries. She walked to the local grocery stores. Even after having the car for over a decade, the mileage on the car was less than 20,000 miles.

My father was also a Do-It-Yourself handyman. If the toilet broke, my father would fix it himself. If the faucet was leaking, he would fix the faucet himself. If roofs leaked, he would climb to the rooftop with a bucket of tar and repair the leak himself. Not only did this cut the cost of hiring someone, it also gave my father experience at fixing things. Thus, it was a win-win situation for him.

These inquisitive and engineering traits later passed on down to my brother and me. He and I would break down broken electronics around the house in an attempt to understand and fix the problem. We learned how to solder wires and repair circuit boards from our father. Our neighbors even started giving us broken electronics for us to fix.

We fixed all of our neighbors' remote controlled cars, television sets, computers, laptops, and even video gaming consoles. We became known on our block as the family that knew how to fix things. And they all came to us, because we never charged them any money. While we believed in saving money, we also did not believe in greed.

Even though my parents only bought me one video game per year, they always gave away video games to our neighborhood kids during their birthdays and during Christmas. So while we were frugal when it came to buying things for ourselves, we were generous when it came to other people. And whenever we got a parking ticket, my mother always said that we should just think of it as a donation to the U.S. government. This mentality of self-sacrifice and generosity was what kept us in control of money and not the other way around. We never let our money control us and dictate our emotions. At no point in our lives did we ever feel that we really needed a large amount of money.

With all of the money we saved, my family invested in my father's herbal store business, in real estate and in mutual funds comprised of stocks and bonds. We never felt poor again, because we knew that we were steadily building a financial nest egg for ourselves in the future. Besides earning money, it is also important to keep the money and make the money work for you.

Lifehack #6: Diversify your investments.

"A fool and his money are soon parted" – Dr. John Bridges

It is easier to think of ways to spend money than it is to think of ways to invest money wisely. There are many stories out there about how celebrities end up bankrupt. People like Nicholas Cage and M.C. Hammer may have been making millions before, but they have struggled with managing their money properly by spending more than they were saving. This is a very common problem among wealthy people who do not properly grasp the concept of investing.

Thus, a man's wealth is not about how many luxurious and unnecessary things he owns. Instead, wealth is measured by how long someone can last in his current lifestyle with just his savings alone. If it is several lifetimes over, then that person is truly wealthy. For the average person, it would only be for a few months.

So where should you invest your money? There's no single safe place to invest your money if you're looking for big returns. For a while, we thought we could safely put our money in stocks. But the Internet bubble in the early 2000's and the recession of 2008 crushed a lot of people's stock portfolios. We thought it was real estate, but housing prices dropped significantly after 2008. We thought it was gold, but even gold sometimes retreats.

That's why we invest in several places. You should never go "all in" with your investments, or you'll suffer what is called, "Gambler's Ruin". The idea behind this is that if you keep gambling all your money against a casino that has infinite money, then you will end up losing all of your money. Even if you win in the beginning, you will lose all of your money over time, because it is a negative sum game. By this I mean that the casino always has a slightly higher chance of winning, so you will lose money in the long run. Therefore, if the person played forever, then the chances of that person losing all of his money would be 100%.

Trading Stocks

A lot of people forget that trading stocks is a negative sum game as well. There are commission fees and ask/buy spreads. Those fees and spreads are often really small, but they do add up over time. Studies have shown that more day traders lose money compared to those who hold onto stocks for at least a month and only trade occasionally. And when it comes to new traders who only trade for a brief period of time and then quit, over 90% of them lose money during that time period (according to a study conducted by Ronald L. Johnson for the North American Securities Administrators Association). That study concluded that a majority of traders were heading towards ruin and bankruptcy if they kept trading in the same way they were trading.

Similar studies have all shown the same results. Terry Odean, a grad student at the University of California Berkeley, and his professor, Brad Barber, researched the accounts of 10,000 discount-brokerage trading accounts from 1987 to 1993. Odean later repeated the study by examining the accounts of 66,465 households from 1991 to 1996. In their studies, they found that as a group, amateur traders were doing poorly versus the market (i.e. they were making less money than if they just bought index stocks).

The reason why amateur traders were doing so poorly was that those traders tend to sell winning stocks too early and hold onto losing stocks for too long. There is a psychological reason for this. When you are holding a losing stock, you tend to not want to sell it, because you'd be admitting to a loss. Nobody likes to admit that they are wrong. So instead, these traders tend to find every excuse to hold onto a stock. They are hoping and praying that the stock will turn around. Then, they end up spending most of their time trying to break even and making more and more emotional trades. The more they traded, the more risk they were putting onto themselves. The studies showed that the more frequent a person trades, the quicker a person loses money and the riskier the account becomes.

On the flip side, if a trader was holding onto a winning stock, they tend to sell it too early. They see a profit and take it immediately. Then as the stock rises, they buy back into the stock, because they don't want to miss out on more profits. However, they tend to buy it back when the stock is at a higher price already. Thus, they already missed out on profits. That loss in profits isn't noticeable to the trader, because they just see it as a missed opportunity. But that loss is truly a loss, because that same trader would hold onto a losing stock and absorb every loss that the stock suffers. This makes their losses larger than their gains.

The other reason why day traders are losing is that they tend to follow what others are doing. When good news about a company comes out, the retail trader just buys the stocks that have already shot up in price. This leaves retail traders with a losing strategy, because they have already missed out on the profits of the stock that shot up. Thus, there is more room for the stock price to decline than to go up further.

Thus, the final conclusions from those trading studies were identical: trading hurts your wealth.

Lifehack #7: Avoid paying for free advice.

Be wary of websites and people trying to sell you tips on stocks or secrets to making money online. Most of these people care more about earning a buck off you than they do about your finances. They can show you their winning trades and show you how much money they won by trading, but they will not show you their losses. What they want is to sell you on the idea that you are missing out on a great opportunity to earn money without working. They want to make money off of you by posing as a guru who knows things that you cannot learn about elsewhere. They will also post "testimonials" or "reviews" on their website to show that real people are actually making money from their advice. This is where you should be cautious. Those testimonials/reviews were either faked or hand-picked. They would never post the negative reviews and testimonials on their own website. And the trading "secrets" that they offer are actually no secrets at all. There is plenty of free trading advice found online already if you really want to dip your toes into trading.

My advice would be to avoid day trading altogether, since it's an emotional roller coaster that will stress you out and waste your time. But if you must try it, then here are some things I learned when I did some day trading in the past. If you are holding onto a winning stock (i.e. a stock that is performing better than the market), then hold onto it until it stops going higher. If you are holding onto a losing stock, then make sure to sell it sooner. Don't ever fall in love with a stock. Once you attach emotions to a stock, you will start making mistakes. The better way to trade would be to set a fixed amount that you're willing to lose and stick to it. Don't ever let a trade make you lose more than 7-8%. Just cut your losses short and move on.

If you want to invest in stocks without day trading, then you should consider putting your money in an index fund. Index funds were created to match the overall market. Thus the price of an index fund is very closely tied to the performance of the overall market. The benefit is that you end up with less analysts and active stock pickers to pay, and thus, you pay lower fees when compared to an actively managed mutual fund. They are also simpler and easier to understand. And since they're passive investments, there are less capital gains taxes to pay and less trading fees to pay. Those things are usually passed onto the fund investors in an actively traded fund.

Your bank's financial adviser will most likely try to get you to invest your money in a mutual fund. There's a reason for this. Take a look at the "front load" of the mutual fund that he or she is recommending. It should be around 2-5%. That's basically what your financial adviser will get paid in commissions if you take his/her "advice" and buy that fund. It is an upfront fee that you pay as soon as you invest your money in the mutual fund. Then there is also an expense ratio, which is the percentage calculated by taking a fund's operating expenses and dividing it by the average dollar value of its assets under management. Those operating expenses are taken directly out of your investment, and could also end up in the pockets of your financial adviser. Always keep this in mind when you speak to him or her. That person may not have your best interests in mind.

Here's a better idea. Set up a Scottrade account (or some other e-trading account) and buy an ETF with your money for just $7 per trade. You can find ETF's that mimic the mutual funds holdings or mimic index funds. If you want to avoid the load fees but still want to join that mutual fund, look to see if that fund has Class D shares. Those usually have no loads, even though the two types of shares are almost identical (Class D shares may have a slightly higher expense ratio). Class A shares (the ones that your financial adviser would push you to get) are the ones with a front load. Class B and C don't have front loads, but they have fees associated with how soon you take out your investment. There's a lot of free education online that teaches you how to invest. And if you really want to learn it in detail, there are cheap investing books you can buy that are written by accomplished investors.

Lifehack #8: Avoid get-rich-quick schemes.

These fee-based advice websites are no different from your typical get-rich-quick website, book or video that promises you "secrets" in exchange for money. The people who make those things tend to misrepresent their wealth in an effort to prove that their "secrets" really work. These are the ones who show off high-end cars, yachts, houses, and make videos about it. They'll talk about how they made thousands of dollars in a day and even show you some Google® AdSense® account statements that "prove" their high income. They'll show you written reviews for their products from "real" people.

But they are faking it in order to sell you their get-rich-quick products. I've been approached many times by these scammers who offered to pay me a few hundred dollars to borrow my exotic cars so that they could make these types of videos. They would also rent a mansion for a few hours and shoot videos of that. All of this was created to give you the illusion that their "secret" system works.

Why would people who make so much money waste time making videos like that? And why would they charge tens or hundreds of dollars for a system that made them millions? It's not worth the time and money. And if it's truly for philanthropy, then why would they not share knowledge for free like many websites do? Why take money from the average Joe when they proclaim to be so wealthy? Why are the reviews for the product found only on their own product page, which they have complete control over? Why not sell the product in the mass market where people can leave reviews on the product without worrying about having their written reviews deleted by the seller? None of it makes sense unless you take into account that their motivation is greed and deceit.

Just remember this before you buy into any more "Get Rich Quick" books: If somebody knows a system where they can get rich quickly, then they'll be using it and not telling you about it.

5 GROWING UP WITH CHESS

My parents raised both my older brother and I in Queens, NY. Like my brother, I went through the public school system and studied hard. I did not want to disappoint my parents, because they worked hard to give me this opportunity. It would have been foolish and irresponsible if I wasted it. Although my father worked from 8 AM to 9 PM, he still spent the night either studying his medical books, teaching me important life lessons, or challenging me at chess. My mother always made sure that we got to school on time, signed us up for extracurricular activities, and limited the amount of TV we watched and video games we played.

Since my TV and video game privileges were limited to only around 3-5 hours a week throughout my entire childhood, I sought out other hobbies to occupy my time. When I was in elementary school, one of those hobbies was playing board games with my family members.

Usually after dinner, my father would be sitting in the living room reading his Chinese newspaper or his books. After I had finished my homework for the night, I would usually challenge him at Xiangqi, which is also known as Chinese chess. Xiangqi is a turn-based strategy board game consisting of two armies with the same goal of defending their fortress while attacking their opponents. My father was hesitant to play against me at first, because I played at a very amateurish level. However, as I played it more and more, I started seeing patterns with the style that my father played. I developed plans to work around his defenses and set up my defenses to counter his attacks. Eventually, I started beating him at the very game that he was trying to teach me.

My father was impressed by my progress at Xiagqi, so he went out to buy an advanced strategy guide. The guide had diagrams of different setups for the pieces on the board, and it would tell you the proper strategy to defend your fortress or to attack your opponent. The purpose of the guide was for the user to practice attack and defense strategies until the user memorized them.

The problem was that I did not have great memory, and my father and I did not play enough that we would memorize the strategies. So instead, we did away with the book and just played by adapting to each other's moves. Eventually, we were playing at around the same level, and I no longer had to bug him in order for him to accept my challenge. Instead, he would be the one coming to my room and asking me to play against him.

While playing with me, he would teach me some of the most important life lessons that I would ever learn. Some of those lessons changed my life forever, and I'm glad he passed that knowledge down to me. Playing chess was actually a setup to one of the most important lifehacks that I would ever learn.

Lifehack #9: Adapt to survive.

I went through three stages when I learned how to play Chinese chess. The first stage was the primitive stage. I did not know what I was doing. I had no strategy or style of playing. I was simply moving pieces on the board instinctually and doing what felt right at the moment. There was little planning involved, because I had not yet learned of all the different checkmate setups. While this method of playing made me unpredictable, it also made me make poorly planned moves. Anyone with a good strategy could have easily defeated me, because of a lot of my moves were wasted.

The second stage was the methodical stage. This was when my father gave me the advanced chess playing strategy guide and taught me all of the common setups that people used to achieve checkmates. While this stage of playing is generally better than the primitive stage of playing, it also made me lose some of my original style of playing. I was no longer unpredictable. My style of playing was very methodical and rigid. Every move I made had a scientific and studied reason for making it. My father knew all of the strategies as well, so he could easily predict which checkmate I was going for. This made it easy for him to defend against the attack strategies that I made. It was a very mechanical process that was determined by one's education on the system.

The third stage was the fluid stage. While I had the knowledge of the different strategies, my style of playing became unpredictable again. By sensing that my attack strategy was already caught by my father, I was able to change up my moves and throw him off-guard. Pretty soon, I was making moves in order to control the pieces that my father was moving. I was playing for both sides and dictating the actions that were going on.

I call this the fluid stage because I no longer have a rigid system of playing. A fluid can take the form of any object it pleases, and can get around hard stone walls by flowing between the cracks or flowing around it. In this case, the hard stone walls are my father's defenses. By adapting on the spot, I could attack in an unpredictable way and defend against any new attack strategies that my father was throwing at me.

Adaption is the key to survival. And you can recognize this three-staged pattern in all aspects of life. Take a person's career for example. If a person starts a job without any experience, he is pretty much just winging it. This is similar to the primitive stage.

If a person is educated, then he will probably become a part of the corporate system. This is the methodical stage. He will have a manager and use his education to complete his job for a fixed salary. And he may someday become a manager himself, but only if he plays within the rules set by the system. This is how corporations are structured. And society as a whole is tailored to push you towards this rigid methodical stage. In this stage, almost every aspect of your life has already been done before and all you have to do is follow the same path. This is the stage most people tend to get stuck in.

I was never content with being in this methodical stage. Things felt too repetitive and uncreative. I felt like I was a mechanical robot that did things according to what I was told and expected to do. Unfortunately, society raised me to be this way. Society expected me to go to school, get a nine-to-five job, and then get married and have kids. This was the so-called "ideal" life. Luckily, I snapped out of it while I was still young, and turned into a maverick.

I owe much of my success to my adoption of new technology. While other programmers were still stuck with the basic programming languages that they were taught in college, I actively sought out new technology and adapted to the changing times. This was the fluid stage of my career. I became my own boss and created innovative things for the PC, the Internet, and iOS devices.

Many have tried starting their own businesses and failed. According to the U.S. government-run Small Business Administration (SBA), seven out of ten new employer firms survive at least 2 years, half at least 5 years, a third at least 10 years, and a quarter stay in business 15 years or more. This means that most businesses fail after five years.

So why do so many businesses fail? A lot of it has to do with businesses that fail to adapt in time. Companies like Apple and Google thrive, because they are always innovating. While companies like Research in Motion® (RIM), which is responsible for the Blackberry®, is failing because it did not embrace new technologies in the smartphone and tablet market in time. And a company like Samsung® is thriving because it is copying Apple's style of innovations. Samsung was sued by Apple successfully for over $1 billion for infringing on Apple's patents in 2012.

So, there are those who innovate and adapt according to market needs (i.e. Apple), those who copy others to survive (i.e. Samsung), and those who fail to copy and adapt in time (i.e. Research in Motion). RIM is pretty much just hoping that people would want their Blackberry phones again without actually reacting to the current market demands. That would be like a dial-up Internet Service Provider surviving solely on their dial-up services without embracing cable, WIFI, or fiber optic technologies. So in the realm of smartphones and tablets, RIM would be stuck in the primitive stage, Samsung would be stuck in the methodical stage, and Apple would be in the fluid stage. Though, all this could change depending on the companies' leadership.

If this was in the realm of artwork, then those in the primitive stage would be the ones with no artwork experience. They would be drawing based on what they thought the artwork should look like. This would lead to really sloppy artwork, unless the person has a natural talent for it. But once the artist gets educated, his artwork becomes clearer and more professional. And when the artist evolves and starts creating his own style of artwork, he enters the fluid stage. In this stage, he is not stuck in any one particular art style that he was educated in. If his art was music, then he would be composing his own style of music rather than simply copying the ones he hears. And if his style is undesired by the market, then he would adapt to what his audience wants while still adding his own creative flair to it.

And if this was a mixed martial arts fight, then those in the primitive stage would be the ones with no fighting experience. They only throw punches instinctually. Those who are in the methodical stage would be using a particular style of fighting and only use moves based on what they learned in that style. Those who are in the fluid stage, have no one particular style, but are also well-versed in many styles. They adapt according to their opponent's fighting style.

So find out which parts of your life are stuck in the primitive or methodical stage. If you are content with routines and consistency, then by all means, stick with the methodical stage. And if you don't wish to bother with learning more, then stay in the primitive stage. But when you want to break out of the constraints of being in a rigid system, then learn to adapt and be formless. Create instead of copy. Only those who choose to break out of the mold are the ones who end up the most successful.

"Be like water making its way through cracks. Do not be assertive, but adjust to the object, and you shall find a way around or through it. Don't get set into one form, adapt it and build your own, and let it grow, be like water. Empty your mind, be formless, shapeless — like water. Now you put water in a cup, it becomes the cup; You put water into a bottle and it becomes the bottle; You put it in a teapot, it becomes the teapot. Now water can flow or it can crash.
Be water, my friend."

– Bruce Lee

6 CLASSMATES

I wasn't the smartest student in my class. There was always someone smarter than me. I wasn't the greatest athlete or the most charming person in class either. I learned early on that there were high chances of someone being better than me at something no matter how great I thought I was. And I saw that as a challenge rather than as an excuse to give up. And on the flip side, I knew that there would always be people who were less fortunate than me. Knowing all of that humbled me.

Even though the people in the cliques in my school mostly hung out with people of their own group, I hung out with people of all different cliques. It didn't matter if a person was hanging out with the cool kids or the nerds; I still hung out with them anyway. And although I came from poor parents, I still hung out with the rich kids in school. And although cliques mostly revolved around ethnicities, I still hung out with students from different ethnicities. There were no boundaries to who I hung out with. I was a nomad amongst the cliques and was never bound to just one group.

I even befriended the people who used to bully me. And there were quite a few kids who tried to bully me. I was always one of the smartest kids in class, so I had a big target on my back for bullies. I've had kids kick me, call me derogatory names, and even stab me. You really had to adapt quickly to survive in the NYC public school system.

But being adaptive doesn't necessarily mean that I had to be two-faced. I still stayed true to myself. Whenever there was an argument between two of my friends, I tried not to take sides. And if I did not have a choice, I'd take arguments from both sides and try to show both sides where the other side was coming from.

Lifehack #10: Don't be divisive. Be open-minded.

If you only choose one side of a hot debate, then you may end up being biased towards the issues. You block out the arguments that go against your side and only focus on the ones that go for your side. And if you associate yourself with a certain group, then you inherit all of the prejudices that are associated with that group.

Take politics for example. Usually those who are close-minded pick a side and never truly accept the arguments from the other side. They tune into news channels that lean towards (and even reinforce) their political views. They are stuck believing in their beliefs, because they have chosen to ignore the arguments against their beliefs. And the more they consume the political bias, the more biased and extreme they become. They start developing a preconceived notion about the other side of politics. Often they think the other side is dumber than the other, or the other side is more hateful than the other. And by associating yourself with either side, people will already judge you before you even get the chance to explain your side of the politics. That is why being open-minded about the issues is a better choice than firmly believing in your political parties' views.

Being open-minded in general can be very useful and rewarding. You learn more this way, and are not stuck believing in something that could potentially be wrong. People will always appreciate it more if you're willing to listen to their side of the argument, instead of being dismissive of what they have to say. And this applies even if the person who wants you to listen is close-minded. And since you don't know if the person is close-minded or not, it is best not to impose your own views onto others without being receptive of the counter-argument.

It is also very hard to be instinctually open-minded, because your ego causes you to always want to be on the right side of the argument. And if you truly believe that you are right, it is hard for your ego to step aside and accept alternative ideas. But think about why you think you are right. Do you only believe it, because of how you instinctually feel or because someone taught you to believe it? If it is either of those reasons, then you should be open to the idea that you might have believed in something that is not true.

When I was younger, I used to think that I was always right while my classmates were wrong. I was among the smarter kids in school, so usually I was right about that assessment. However, after I went to college, I was surrounded by people who were just as smart as I was. It was hard for me to break my old habit of always believing that I was right. So, I used to be stubborn and close-minded whenever there was an argument.

I finally got the wake-up call after having a long shouting contest with my close college friend over a science problem (something that only nerds do). Later on, I realized that I was the one who was wrong the entire time. I felt really stupid for not really listening to her arguments. I physically listened, but it did not penetrate into my cerebral cortex. Something had to change with the way I approached arguments.

One of the reasons for my early close-mindedness was that I was raised to be a skeptic. I've been scammed a few times when I was really young. When you're young, you tend to be trusting of people and tend to be more gullible. I've also been surrounded by people who claimed to be right, but were later proven to be wrong. This led me to be skeptical about anything anyone says to me.

I slowly grew out of my close-mindedness as I found time after time again that my ideas may not have been the best ones. My ego wanted me to believe that I was always in the right, but I quickly learned to ignore my ego after having many humbling experiences with people who were smarter and more educated than I was.

So how do you overcome your close-mindedness?

Don't identify yourself by your thoughts and beliefs. When Neil deGrasse Tyson, astrophysicist and director of the Hayden Planetarium, was asked whether he was an atheist or not, he replied with a response that summed up my philosophy pretty well:

"The only 'ist' I am is a scientist… I don't associate with movements. I'm not an 'ism'. I just – I think for myself. The moment when someone attaches to a philosophy or a movement, then they assign all the baggage and all the rest of the philosophy that goes with it to you. And when you want to have a conversation, they will assert that they already know everything important there is to know about you because of that association. And that's not the way to have a conversation. I'm sorry. It's not. I'd rather we explore each other's ideas in real time rather than assign a label to it and assert, you know, what's going to happen in advance."

– Neil deGrasse Tyson

My skepticism led me to become an atheist when I was just a teenager. I was raised as a Christian, because my mother was a firm believer in Christianity. I even attended church every Sunday against my will until around high school. After studying science and taking a hard look into Christianity and other religions, I realized that religion was an unproven belief system. Religion, along with most of the stories associated with religion, made no sense to me. It went against logic and reasoning.

That's when I started to associate myself with atheism. It was a reaction to feeling scammed and lied to. I went to the opposite extremity to distance myself as far as possible from what I believed at the time were fairy tales told to people to make them feel better about themselves for doing righteous things and shameful for doing unethical things. I saw it as a tool for kings to socially engineer his people into doing the things he wanted them to do without questioning his authority (which he would claim came from God himself). With this belief in mind, I saw it as my rightful duty to stop people from falling for this lie.

I have had many heated debates with my mother and brother about this issue, because they were both firm believers of Christianity. And the debates always ended up diminishing my relationship with them. But, my ego was pushing me to further pursue the issue until they believed what I believed in. I honestly believed that they were being scammed, and that I was their savior. But what were the end results? They are still believers of Christianity, and nothing really progressed.

My mother once asked me, "If religion makes me feel happy, then why would you want to take that happiness away?" After that, I realized what the purpose of religion was to most people. It was no longer just about maintaining control over the masses. Religion was a tool used by people in terrible situations to cope with their lives. After this epiphany, I stopped forcing my beliefs onto them and others.

A study by Frank Sulloway and Michael Shermer had shown that a person's belief in religion decreased with age until around the age of seventy-five when it shot up again. Because of this strange uptick in religious beliefs after the age of seventy-five, they postulated that a person's age was not the cause of one's religious beliefs. Rather, a person's age strongly correlated with his or her situation, and the situation was what determined a person's religious beliefs. For example, an elderly woman was more likely to have lost power, status and loved ones at her age. Along with a perceived impeding death, this woman would more likely turn to religion to help her cope.

Thus, forcing one's beliefs onto others is not the way to go. You may introduce your ideas and hypotheses to them, but it is ultimately up to them to choose what they believe in. That's a freedom that everyone is entitled to.

If I kept pushing my beliefs onto others, then I would be no better than the religious people who did the same. My mother had been through a rough life. And if religion helped her recover from that life, then I should not stop her from believing in it.

After I learned to ignore my ego, I decided that being an agnostic was more fitting of my philosophy. An agnostic is a person who believes that it is impossible to know of the existence or nature of God or of anything beyond material phenomena. The atheists I know are actively against those who believe in a God or believe in spiritualism. You see them on internet message boards all of the time. If there's a YouTube video that deals with something even remotely religious, you will see a debate between atheists and religious people. It would be nice to see a healthy debate on the issue so that we could further each other's knowledge. But, this was not what I was seeing. What I saw were two bickering sides that wouldn't budge on their beliefs. The net outcome was just anger and hatred on both sides as well as strained relations.

That is why I am taking the stance that I don't know whether there is a God or not. If clear scientific evidence presents itself for either side, then I am ready to embrace it and further my knowledge. But in the meantime, I will not claim superiority in knowing something that I do not actually have proof of. And if given the choice, I would rather not even talk about religion to people, because I do not want to spend my free time talking about such divisive things. I rather focus on bringing people together rather than dividing them.

Instead of arguing about religion, we should focus on furthering one's knowledge of the world every day and on helping the people around the world suffer less. And if your religion covers those two basic philosophies, then we're already on the same page. And if more of us weeded out the details of our religions, we would probably realize that the religions we follow mostly have the same running theme of self-enlightenment, and helping the less fortunate. And then hopefully, we'll realize that we're all human beings under the same Sun with roughly the same goals. We just so happen to be slightly different from each other.

But realistically, peaceful coexistence will probably never exist. Different personalities lead to differing opinions. So, what may seem great to you may not seem so great to someone else. This is why it is important to keep an open-mind about everyone's opinions.

Lifehack #11: Embrace your haters.

Behind every successful person, there lies someone who hates him for being successful or hates what he does.

I had haters even early on in my life. One of those haters ripped my name tag off of an artwork that I spent months drawing. It was so well drawn that it ended up in the front lobby of my high school. Someone at my school didn't like that. And the fact that it was my name that was ripped off made it clear that it was a personal attack.

Haters are just another incarnation of bullies. And I always find that the easiest way to get bullies to stop bullying you is to get to know them and befriend them. I knew that there was a reason for their anger towards me, and usually it's because they were dimwitted, jealous, and/or came from a broken family. A lot of the bullies had parents who were divorced. This left them with an alpha male attitude, because they grew up without loving parents to coddle them. They learned to fend for themselves and probably held much anger towards society for not giving them a better life. Without the proper guidance, this usually led them to express their anger in displays of dominance and strength in order to gain validation from others.

And then there are the bullies who have parents who spoil them. These are usually wimps in a real life fight, but their snobbish and condescending attitude towards others is no different from physical bullying. These are the kids who call people derogatory names and get away with it, because they don't receive retaliation for it. Usually it's when they themselves get knocked down a few pegs, do they ever stop their bullying.

Thus, most of the battle is won by getting to know your enemy. By relating to people, you learn to speak to them in a way that makes them want to be your friend rather than your enemy. This is why I had to be a chameleon in order to befriend the people in the different groups.

Sometimes, to stop the haters, you really just have to stop doing what they hate you for. At a young age, I used to brush off criticism for my work, because I was still egotistical and thought that my work were masterpieces. Eventually, I learned to accept constructive criticism and even welcome it. Criticism helped me grow because it showed me more about what the markets wanted. Now when people offer suggestions and criticism for my products, I listen.

Nowadays, I don't have many haters in my life, because I left them with nothing to really hate on. I was once hated for being arrogant and egotistical, but now I try to be humble and modest. I was once hated for showing off my wealth, but now I try to hide my wealth as much as possible. Instead of fighting the haters and giving them more fuel, sometimes it's better to just take away the fuel and leave them with nothing to hate you for.

Lifehack #12: Know your enemies and know your market.

Since I was such a big target for bullies, I had to adapt to survive the school system. Knowing how to interact with different people from different backgrounds is the key to good marketing. Your social skills will translate to better sales. And they are especially important if you want to create good business connections.

I know many programmers, IT technicians, and web developers who are great at what they do. They can arguably code better than I can. But they lack the social skills necessary to create good business connections. There can be a number of reasons for this. They are sometimes condescending, and they cannot relate with the common man. They see regular people as inferior for not understanding technology, and therefore do not bother interacting with them. Sometimes it's because they spend so much time at their computers coding that they do not spend enough time socializing with their classmates after school. Sometimes it's because the parts of their brains that deals with logic and reasoning (important skills required for coding) have been so developed, that it causes the part of their brain that is responsible for socializing to be underdeveloped. And finally, sometimes it's because programmers don't have fashion sense, and/or they're seen as not cool. Thus, their classmates shun them, and they don't get to socialize even if they try.

When I started high school, I was a part of this group of computer geeks who didn't socialize that much. I went to a specialized high school that required you to pass an exam to get in. Only a few people from my junior high school got in. Thus, I didn't know that many people at the school, and everyone kept mostly to their own cliques.

The only people I socialized with regularly were the other socially awkward kids at school. I was a pretty shy kid when I was younger – possibly because I was small in stature and thus lacked confidence.

And my shyness made it hard for me to make the effort to speak to others. The other kids at school also saw me as a nerd (yes, even in a school full of smart kids), and thus I wasn't considered one of the "cool" ones.

That all changed when my best female friend in high school started going out with my best male friend in high school. I was deeply attracted to her, because she was one of the few prettier girls who bothered to speak with me, even though I was a vertically-challenged Asian nerd. And both of them knew that I was attracted to her. Needless to say, that relationship broke my 16-year-old heart, and that's when I knew that things had to change.

By the time this all happened, I had a pretty good grade point average in my high school. Thus, I knew that I could afford to give up some of my time spent studying in exchange for time spent socializing with other people. Shifting my focus away from school and more towards socializing did lower my grades, but it was worth it. It helped me develop better communication skills later on, and allowed me to understand people more.

One of the first things I had to change was the way I presented myself. I had always been dressed by my mother, who had horrible fashion sense. She picked clothes based on how cheap they were rather than how good they looked. I ended up wearing a lot of bootleg Mickey Mouse shirts and other embarrassing pieces of clothing. But she grew up in the ghetto, so I couldn't blame her. The worst of all the nerd accessories I had was the pair of granny glasses that I sported throughout high school. Even though I was only nearsighted, I wore big glasses that could fit bifocal lenses. I ditched those for contact lenses in my fashion transformation. I later got laser eye surgery to fix my vision permanently.

I also started buying my own clothing using the money I earned from my summer jobs. I chose clothes based on what the cool kids were wearing, but I also changed it up enough to create my own style. My hair used to be a mess as well. In an effort to save money, my mother only took me to the barber once every two months or so. I ended up sporting a small afro, because my hair was naturally spiky and I wasn't cutting it often enough. To change this, I started going to a better barbershop and styling my hair with gel. This was my way of adapting to the very superficial and critical world of high school students.

This entire transformation happened over the summer between junior year and senior year. And the transformation was quite astonishing. People at my school no longer recognized me. Even my own cousins did not recognize me at family gatherings. The transformation was so drastic that the senior girls on my school bus, who rode with me for three years prior, had asked me who I was. I ended up dating several girls that year, even though I never had a girlfriend in the previous years.

This experience was my first lesson in marketing. In this case, it was marketing my own image. My character never changed. I was still the same person as before. The only difference was my presentation. I exuded confidence.

This was a lesson to teach me to get to know my market. I had to give them what they wanted in order for me to get what I wanted. And having just good content or a good product was not enough, because first impressions were important. When you buy a bag of dog food, do you look at the packaging or do you taste the food to see if it's good? Most of the time, you'd buy a product based on its packaging.

On the other hand, most people get turned off by a product because of how poorly made their packaging is. If the packaging is bad, you start questioning the quality of the product inside. Thus, presentation is what a lot of the app developers need to learn.

App development tip #1: Presentation is key.

I often see many great apps in the app market that don't do well in sales. The problem is that they lack presentation. Potential customers are already turned off by the icon, so they don't even bother tapping on the app details to investigate the app further.

I once developed an app called "Cop Radio" to prove that presentation was important. The icon was a very vague black icon with the white/blue letters 'C' and 'R' on it. The icon looked very good, but it didn't really tell the user what was in the app. The download rate for the app was in the hundreds per day, but nowhere as impressive as I had hoped.

Unsatisfied with the sales, I changed the icon to a bright blue color with the words "Police Scanner+" on it. I also changed the name of the app to "Police Scanner+". The app itself did not change at all. It was still the same app underneath. Yet, the download rate was now in the thousands per day instead of the hundreds. It shot up to being one of the top 10 most downloaded news apps in the App Store in 2012, when Cop Radio barely broke the top 100.

Let my experience be a lesson that the icons and screenshots are some of the most important marketing tools you have for selling your app. And I am sure that this applies across all businesses. Although many of you probably knew that presentation was important, you probably did not know how important it was. I certainly didn't.

I was taught from movies that personality and the content of a character was the most important in getting girls to like you. This was probably true if we were looking at a long term relationship. But, in order for someone to even notice you, you have to look approachable and decent first; then she'll give you a chance to show off your awesome personality. And in the realm of the App Store, icons and screenshots are in the forefront of presenting your apps.

There are many cases where people buy apps based on just the icon and screenshots alone. They don't even bother reading the reviews or description. There was a brief period of time in the App Store when there were apps being sold as "cell phone trackers". The premise was that you would enter a person's phone number, and the app would tell you where the phone was. In the icon, it showed an image of a radar screen like the one you would see in a submarine. In the screenshots, it showed a place to enter a phone number, and then showed a map rendering of where that phone was located. Both the icons and screenshots were very professionally made.

While that would have been a really nifty app, the actual app did not work as you would have assumed. In the description, it said something along the lines of, "This is for entertainment purposes. The app will prank your friends into thinking that it works, but it only shows your own location when you enter any number." Nobody bothered reading the description. If they did, then they would have figured out that it did not work in the manner that they assumed. And in the reviews, there were thousands of negative reviews saying that they felt ripped off and that they should have read the description or reviews first before buying the app.

Those apps ended up in the Top 100 paid apps list for the App Store and made thousands of dollars. This may have been an extreme case, but this goes to show that presentation can be more important than the content of the product itself. And this was not an anomaly. There were other apps that had misleading screenshots and icon. For example, there was once a string of apps that made you think that you could lock and unlock your iPhone using your fingerprint. Obviously, this was impossible, because the iPhone did not have the necessary fingerprint scanning hardware on the screen. But a lot of people still bought the app anyway. The presentation was there, and they fell for it.

And if you think that this was a great way to make money, then think again. Most of these deceiving apps don't last longer than a month in the Top 100 list of top paid apps. To stay in the Top 100, your app had to be both presentable and have great content. My "5-0 Radio" police scanner app stayed in the Top 100 paid and Top 100 free apps for over two years, because it had both the presentation and content to back it up. If the content was bad, the success of my 5-0 Radio app would not have lasted longer than a month. Instead of making the millions of dollars that it made, it would have only made a few thousands of dollars.

7 COMPUTER SCIENCE

I chose computer science (C.S.) as one of my majors, because I had already been making websites and coding C++ and Java programs in high school. I created my first website in junior high school and learned how to build my own computer even before that. As a child, I was always curious about how things worked, so I would take things apart and put them back together. That was how I learned to build my own computer, and why I also majored in computer engineering. I was one of the first people on the internet back when I was still in elementary school. And I was also one of the first people in my school to have his own website.

Because our family used to be so poor, my brother and I used to go around the neighborhood during trash day and pick up computers that people had thrown away. We would salvage parts from the computer and either use them as spare parts or add it to our existing computers. I did not even get to buy my own computer until I was in high school. To this day, I still build my own computers and try to stay on the cutting edge of technology by learning and adopting new technologies on my own.

My family's first computer was a Commodore® 64. Even before I knew what "load" meant, I was typing commands into the Commodore 64 and running video games that my brother borrowed from his friends. To learn how to use the Commodore 64, I watched what my brother did, and it intrigued me.

Eventually my brother bought a computer with a Windows® operating system and got himself a dial-up modem. Before there was even the World Wide Web, my brother and I would attach the phone line to the computer to join what were called Bulletin Board Systems (BBS).

A Bulletin Board System is a computer system running software that allows users to connect and log in to the system using text commands. Think of it as a message board that you have to call directly from your computer to send and get messages. My brother used BBSes to download new software (such as demos for video games), chat with friends, and get updates on his friends. It was a precursor to the World Wide Web, and social networking websites.

Eventually, my brother got AOL® on his computer, because his best friend loaned him his AOL account. We were too poor to afford having an internet subscription, so we didn't even pay for Internet access until I was a senior in high school. After my brother's friend stopped loaning us his AOL account, I used a free internet service called NetZero®, which allowed you to go online in exchange for viewing advertisements. When I got my first email account during elementary school, I was excited to even receive one new email. I used to sign up for newsletters just so I'd get daily emails. I remember that the first thing I did after I came back from school was check to see if I got any new emails. Nowadays, I try to minimize the number of emails I get, and actually enjoy it more when I don't get emails.

Since the computer was in my brother's room, I usually had to sneak in there to use it. My brother didn't like me being in his room. So every time I wanted to use the computer, I had to turn into a covert-ops agent and sneak my way into his room without anyone noticing. When I heard him coming, I quickly hid in his closet or behind the door.

This kind of taboo behavior around the computer only piqued my interest more. When I finally got my own computer in junior high school, it was like discovering Pandora's Box. It was the old computer that my brother was using before he won a laptop from a raffle. But, it didn't matter to me that it was old and slow. I wanted to learn everything I could about the machine, and the internet was my guide to everything.

I created my very first website in the 7th grade. All of the other websites looked pretty bad back then with their animated flaming gifs, Times New Roman black font and blue under-lined links. People didn't know how to code websites back then, so they all used website templates or "What You See Is What You Get" (WYSIWYG) HTML editors. A WYSIWYG HTML editor basically hides all of the website coding and lets you create websites by simply dragging and dropping the elements you want onto the WYSIWYG editor. I wanted full control over the codes of my websites, so I learned how to code a whole website by hand without using a WYSIWYG editor. To this day, I still don't use WYSIWYG editors much. Just using a basic text-editor was good enough for me.

High School

Throughout my school years, I had trouble taking English tests. Since my memory wasn't that great, I had trouble memorizing vocabulary words. English was also my second language, and people only spoke Chinese in my house. Also my parents didn't buy me any English books, and the nearest library was too far from my house. Thus, all of these disadvantages meant that I wasn't very good at taking any English exams.

When I took the NYC high school entrance exam, which tested middle school students on Math and English, I had only been accepted to the second best high school in New York City, Bronx High School of Science. I was only one correct answer away from being accepted into Stuyvesant High School, the #1 high school in NYC. Because of my financial disadvantage and high exam score, the New York City Board of Education offered to allow me attend Stuyvesant High School if I attended a summer school. I opted out, because I did not want to be one of the dumbest students in that school.

By choosing to go to Bronx Science, I was among the top

students going there. My 96% GPA was among the top student GPA's of the school and it could have been higher if I didn't get distracted during my senior year there. Although I did not get to be valedictorian or salutatorian, they did give me a school award that had a large college scholarship attached to it. Only one student per year won that award. For my financial background, having the extra cash to pay for college was a better award than being valedictorian.

By having less competition and challenge in high school, I had more free time to learn other things. After I had mastered HTML during my freshmen year, I moved onto learning Flash. Back then, all of the cool websites had Flash in it. It's a bit archaic now to have Flash on your website, but it was the fad of the late 1990's and early 2000's. The ability to add more interactivity to your website that normal HTML and JavaScript couldn't do was what fascinated me the most. This fascination ultimately led me to develop apps, where good interactivity was one of the main selling points.

During my junior year, my high school started offering C++ classes. It was a very basic class that taught me the fundamentals of programming. It was in that class that I found out that I had a talent for programming. I learned C++ at a much faster pace than everyone else did. While my memory skills were not excellent, my logic, critical thinking, creativity and mathematical skills made up for it. All of those were essential to learning how to program code.

I aced every exam given in that class, and I also did all of the extra credit work. I didn't have to, but I wanted the challenge anyway. I eventually got bored with how slow the class was going, so I skipped several chapters ahead. Once I finished with the entire textbook, I decided to have some fun in the class, because there were still some months left in the semester.

Lifehack #13: Don't boast. You can trust no one.

The computers with the Windows 95 operating system that my C++ class had were easily hacked. I played pranks on the other students by modifying their Windows splash screen to show random pictures of celebrities. I had written a batch file that would automate the entire process. All I had to do was put in the floppy disk with my hack, and run the autoexec.bat file. The whole hack took less than a few seconds. So when the class started or finished, I'd put the hack in before the students took their seats. Since the teacher had no idea how to change the splash screen back, I was able to infect several computers with my prank before they were all changed back.

The one mistake I had was that I had the stupid idea of attaching my alias to the images. I wanted credit for my work, just like how graffiti artists wrote their name on their work. Eventually, someone recognized my alias and snitched on me to the C.S. teacher.

The teacher confronted me after class was over and said, "Someone told me that you were the one behind this. I don't care if you did or didn't do it. Just change it back, and I will not tell the dean about this."

Later that week, I snuck into the empty computer room during a bathroom break in another class. I changed it all back while making sure that nobody was looking. The teacher kept his promise and never told the dean about it. But I later learned that my prank did not go unpunished.

When you apply to college, you have the option to select one school for an early-decision application. This meant that you promised to attend the school if they accepted you. The idea was that if you were on the borderline of being accepted, the school would accept you if they saw that you were an early-decision applicant. Colleges don't like their acceptance letters to be rejected, so they prefer early-decision applications.

I applied to an Ivy League school as my early-decision college choice. But, my application was marked incomplete because one of my two recommendation letters was not received by the school. When I asked around, I found out that it was my C.S. teacher's recommendation letter that was never sent out. I only chose him to write my recommendation, because I was applying to the school as a computer science major. I had other teachers as back-up if he didn't want to do it. But he promised that he would do it, so I trusted him.

That ultimately screwed me over, because he either forgot to do it, or he was punishing me for the prank I pulled. To this day, I still don't know why he didn't mail that recommendation letter in time. Either way, his letter must not have been that great, because when I reapplied as a normal applicant a month later, I was wait-listed. And for every school that didn't require a recommendation letter, I was accepted.

Perhaps it was for the best that I didn't end up in that Ivy League school. I saved tens of thousands of dollars in tuition by attending a public school instead of an Ivy League school. Also, by having a less challenging workload at my non-Ivy League school, I was able to do a lot of self-education on the side.

Lifehack #14: Take advantage of free education.

After my C++ class, I wanted to use my newfound skills in the real world. So I found a summer internship that was being offered to just one candidate at a tech company in Manhattan. The company focused on creating Java-based web solutions and IT consulting for different small business and corporate clients. Their biggest client was for a pharmaceutical corporation that created a famous allergy medicine. It seemed like a company that would help me get a foot in the door, so I applied for the internship.

During the interview, various employees and even the CEO of company interviewed me. The CEO said that I showed promise because of my high SAT scores and because of my perfect grade in my computer science class. But the problem he had with me was that I only knew how to code in C++ when the job requirement was for Java, a similar, but different programming language. So he told me to reapply when I knew how to code in Java.

I took him up on the offer and quickly went to the library after the interview was over. At the library, I borrowed a book that taught the basics of Java. I started reading it as though I had an exam on the matter the next day. After reading the book for many hours straight, I decided that I knew enough about Java to reapply for the job. So I called up the CEO of the company the next day and told him that I learned Java and would like a second chance at the internship. He was curious, so he granted me that second chance.

During the second interview, they asked me a few basic questions about Java, and I knew the answers. However, as the interview went on, the questions got more advanced, and I didn't know the answers. I tried to answer them in the best way that I could, but they weren't the right answers.

After the interview was over, the CEO said, "You didn't answer all of the interview questions correctly. Next time, just say that you don't know the answer instead of giving a bad answer. It's okay to not know the answers sometimes. What intrigued me the most about you was that I told you to come back when you knew Java, and you actually went out and tried to learn Java. You didn't wait a year or a month or even a week to start learning. You went out and tried it immediately. You may not be the best Java coder we interviewed, but you definitely have the attitude that I would like to see in my employees. I'm going to accept you for the internship. But I want you to review those Java books some more."

And that was when I got my first job at a tech company.

The learning curve at the company was very steep. I had to learn new technologies, such as Apache, SOAP, REST, Java, Linux, JavaScript, UNIX, and VI, at the internship. Since the other employees were busy with their own work, they only told me what to learn without actually teaching me anything. I had to learn everything on my own.

It was all overwhelming at first, but the challenge of it all was what kept me pushing to learn more. I was basically learning college level material while I was interning there. One of the employees told me that spending a month there was equal to spending a semester in college.

All of the technologies I learned at the internship would later prove useful when I had a web development course in college, and when I was interviewed for tech jobs. Although the steep learning curve would have deterred most people from wanting to move forward and learn more, it ultimately benefited me. I stood out during my college applications and during my job interviews.

One of the major differences between humans and animals is that we can share knowledge easily and learn things faster than animals can. Why should we throw this talent away? Educate yourself beyond what is expected of you, and you will be rewarded in the long run.

"Continuous effort - not strength or intelligence - is the key to unlocking our potential."

– Winston Churchill

8 UGLY WORLD

From all of the bullies and gangsters at my school, I already knew how ugly the world was out there. It was pretty much a dog eat dog world. It seemed like almost every day there was someone trying to scam you.

I was even scammed by an older classmate when I was in the first grade. Back then, I used to make and sell paper ninja stars for a dime each. None of my classmates knew how to make them, but they thought the ninja stars were the coolest things they've ever seen. One day, a classmate who was a year older than us told me that he would pay 50 cents for each of my ninja stars. But he said that I'd have to let him try out my paper ninja stars at home first before he would pay me the next day. So he took my whole box of a dozen or so ninja stars with him home. He ended up never paying for them. When I asked him about the money, he would always find an excuse to explain why he didn't have it. I trusted him, because I was gullible at that age. My brother had to explain to me later on that I'd just been scammed.

And when I got on the internet, there were even more scams. I had my first major experience with an online scam back when I was a teenager. It involved a web-based game called Neopets®.

One of the biggest crazes during my time in high school was online multiplayer games. Neopets became very popular at my school. You basically control a virtual pet, and you must play Flash games to gain money to buy food and clothes for your pet. There was even a store interface that you could set up to sell your in-game items for in-game currency. It was through these customizable stores that people were scamming victims.

Lifehack #15: Use social engineering to get what you want.

The creators of Neopets were ignorant enough to allow HTML tags for your store. They even allowed you to add custom cascading style-sheets (CSS). So scammers of the game would sell high-valued items at low prices to attract unsuspecting victims to their Neopets store. But they also hid their actual store using CSS, and created a fake store made out of HTML. If you clicked on the fake store item in an attempt to try to buy it, you were taken to an external website that resembled the login page for the Neopets website. After the victim enters his username and password into the fake login page, the scammer can use that info to log into the victim's account.

The whole setup is what computer security professionals called 'Phishing'. It is a play on the word 'fishing', because the whole setup resembles a person laying out bait and fishing for what he wants (and in this case, Neopets accounts). What the Neopets scammer would do next was log into the victim's account, buy cheap items from his own account's store at ridiculously high prices, and then create a fake shop for the victim's account to reel in even more victims. This allowed the scammer to transfer a lot of in-game currency from the victim's account to his own account. The whole setup could be repeated over and over again with increasingly higher success rates as more and more fake shops were being set up.

The hack was pretty interesting to me because it was more of a social engineering hack than a computer hack. It relied more on the hacker's ability to deceive the human mind rather than his ability to find vulnerabilities in a programmer's code. I studied this type of social engineering extensively and mastered it myself. The ability to convince a massive number of people to do what you want without them knowing that they are being manipulated proved to be quite useful later on. It was actually a lot like how chess players tried to convince their opponents to move their pieces in a certain way without them knowing that they were being influenced into doing so.

The 1% Rule

I never fell for these scams, but I learned that there were many naïve people out there who would. That gave me the confidence to believe that given a large enough sample size, there was bound to be someone who would do what you wanted him to do. I called it the 1% rule.

The 1% rule is simply my theory that about 1% or more of people in a large enough sample size will do exactly the opposite of what everyone else is doing. Take movie ratings for example. Even if a movie is universally praised by a majority of critics, there will always be a few reviews that say that the movie is horrible. And you can even see this 1% rule occur during the U.S. elections. While a majority of people vote for either Democrats or Republicans, there's always that small percentage of people who votes for a third party. Even though the odds are very stacked against them for the third candidate to win the election, they still use their vote to vote for that third candidate.

App development tip #2: Position your ads carefully.

You can actually make money off of this rule. By placing banner advertisements in strategic locations on your website, you can get ad revenue when 1% of the people clicks on the banner advertisements.

The best location I found on a mobile website is a banner at the very top of the page. When I ran my company's regoapps.com website with just a few banner ads at the bottom, the ad revenue was not that great. But when I added a banner to the very top, my ad revenue more than doubled. I verified this strategy when I made the same changes to the mobile website of a photo-sharing company that I co-owned. The changes doubled the ad revenue overnight.

On a mobile app, I found that the best location is at the very bottom of the app. Sometimes people need to reach the very top of their phone's screen with their thumbs while they are holding their phone. The bulging flesh at the bottom of their thumbs tends to touch the bottom-right of the screen when they reach for the top of the screen with their thumb (or bottom-left corner if they are holding it with their left hand).

Another trick I learned to double the ad revenue on the mobile ads was to put a "close" or "hide" button on the top-right of the ad banner. You should not be covering the ad itself or else you'd be violating some ad network policies. But it should be small enough and close enough to the banner to cause users to accidentally tap the banner ads. But be careful when you use this method, as Google does not like it when their banner ads are tapped by accident. In fact, they would ban you or your company for life if there are too many accidental clicks to their banner ads. And if you try to appeal it, they will just give you a robotic answer denying your request for a second chance. That's why I would avoid using Google's ad networks if you want to employ this trick.

One of the other tricks I learned is to become an affiliate for iTunes®, Amazon® and other websites. For those who don't know, affiliate marketing is where a company pays you commission for helping them sell their products. You can make extra revenue just by putting links to the company's products on your website or app. As long as people are clicking on the link, there is bound to be a percentage of people who will then proceed to buy something. And for each sale, you earn a percent of the purchase price. I've been making a lot of money from the affiliate links that I put on my website and my apps, so I can tell you that it's worth it. It's not so much that it is giving me millions of dollars, but it's a decent amount of money that will make it worth your while. That's in stark contrast to zero affiliate revenue if I haven't put those links in. And there is very little work in putting a link on your website or app.

Affiliate marketing is something that a lot of those "make money online" e-books teach you to do. However, there is not really much secret magic behind it, and it will not make you rich quickly (unless your website or app gets millions upon millions of visitor hits). Just do your research on where to sign up for affiliate links, and there, they will give you instructions on how to link to certain products with your affiliate link. So if your website is related to jazz music, you may want to link to some jazz songs. And if your website is related to apps, then you may want to link to some apps. This is what is called 'targeted advertising', because you're giving your target audience certain advertisements based on what they enjoy. Even if you link to your apps on iTunes, you can earn commission off those sales. That way, you'd really be earning 75% of the sale instead of the usual 70% that Apple gives you.

That's pretty much all you need to know about affiliate marketing. A more detailed analysis on affiliate marketing can be found by searching on your favorite search engine for more information. Keep in mind that most educational material can be found for free online these days, so dishing out money is not required. The people hawking those "get rich from working at home" e-books are really just making the majority of their income from the e-book sales, and not really from their affiliate marketing tricks. If a person has a good strategy, then that person would more likely spend his or her time trying to grow that method of making money instead of trying to share it with other people.

9 COLLEGE

For college, I chose to attend UCLA (University of California, Los Angeles) and majored in Computer Science and Engineering. I had always wanted to live in Los Angeles after having been there for a few months when I was younger. The weather was great, the restaurants were world-renowned, and the people were laid back. The other top colleges were in the middle of nowhere, and just studying all day didn't seem like my ideal college experience.

I'd also be lying if I said that the vast number of beautiful girls at UCLA wasn't a major selling point for me and my hormonal self. My brother, who got his B.S. from Carnegie Mellon University (CMU), told me that I shouldn't expect to meet a lot of girls at CMU if I chose to go there. It was ranked as the number one computer science school, but the male to female ratio there was three to two. That wasn't very appealing.

But besides the allure of attractive girls, UCLA was the birthplace of the internet and one of the top computer science schools in the world. Some of UCLA's course material was taken straight from Massachusetts Institute of Technology's open-course material. So, the things that I was learning at UCLA were similar to the things I would have learned at M.I.T. I figured that if there was anything else I wanted to learn, I could have learned it on my own.

By having less competition in my classes, I was able to spend more time self-educating myself rather than studying material that I would probably never use in a real-life career. For example, since the many years that I've graduated from UCLA, I have never been required to flip through my advanced calculus notes to figure out how to deal with a real-world problem. Perhaps if I was in a career where advanced calculus was needed, then I would probably be glad that I learned it. But, college tends to teach more than you need to know (presumably to milk as much tuition out of you as possible). They, of course, would call it expanding your general knowledge of the world. I would call it a waste of my time and money. Luckily, UCLA was a public school and a relaxing one, so my wasted time and money was minimized. This opened up the opportunity for me to start my hobby of online game hacking.

Online Game Hacking

During my freshmen year in college, there was a Korean game called GunBound® that grew popular among Asian-Americans. GunBound was a free online multiplayer game, where you choose a tank and fight against other people in teams of four. Every player takes turns trying to destroy the tanks on the other team. You earned in-game gold for every kill and win you got, and you could power up your character by buying equipment using the in-game gold.

My best friend and I were late adopters to the game, so we were constantly being crushed by my friends from high school, because they had better equipment. She and I worked really hard to earn the gold to catch up to our friends. But each time we tried to catch up, they would progress more in the game as well.

This was around the time when I started learning how to read and modify assembly language (ASM), which is a low-level programming code where each statement corresponds to machine code. Machine code is the actual set of instructions that you give a CPU to do the task given. In comparison, C++ and Java are high-level programming languages that convert your simple statements into complex machine code. But coding in assembly language meant that you were coding every line of machine code yourself.

The reason why this is significant is because when programs are running, they get stored in the RAM as machine code. Thus, to reverse engineer a computer program, you would have to understand the machine code that was written. And by understanding how the game code works, you can modify the machine code in the RAM to get the game to do what you want it to do.

In GunBound, for example, there must be a piece of game code that tells your computer that your character lost health after getting hit. By modifying that game code, you can get your computer to think that you never got hit and therefore would never lose health. This would have been easy game hack to do if this were an offline game. However, since all the computers playing in the same game had to be in sync, you would get kicked out of the game if your health reading did not match up with the health readings from the rest of the players.

Therefore, it was a challenge to hack this game, and nobody really knew how to do it. I took up that challenge, because it seemed fun to search for the vulnerabilities in the game code and hack the game to my advantage.

One of the first hacks I found for the game was an innocent one. It allowed you to bypass the vulgar language filter, and allowed you to swear in the in-game chat without it turning into a mash of asterisks and punctuation marks. I shared the hack among my friends so that we could speak freely amongst one another without ever being filtered again. But, I never told them that I was the one who made it. I also distributed the hack freely on a new blog I created.

Since I valued my anonymity, I created that blog under a false alias named Janette. The picture I used for my alias was a picture of a cute blonde girl, whose photo I found from some random website. I maintained that alias until the closure of that blog. Although I could have attached my name to the blog, I had put my ego aside in exchange for my privacy.

Eventually, I discovered more fun hacks that the game developers did not block. I created a hack that allowed users to modify the trajectory of their opponents' missiles by changing the gravity and wind physics in the game. This led to some hilarious scenarios where people shot themselves. After seeing how fun it was to modify the game, I spent more time exploring the game code and figuring out new ways to hack the game.

Another hack I made, which I nicknamed "act of Zeus", allowed you to shoot an unlimited number of lightning bolts from the sky at anywhere you chose. The ability to shoot one lightning bolt per round usually only occurred after you died (sort of like a revenge attack), and each bolt did very little damage. However, I hacked the game code to allow me to shoot as many lightning bolts as I wanted, even though it wasn't my turn and I wasn't dead. This meant that I could blast anyone into smithereens at any given time during the game.

Having that kind of power at a young age, even in a video game, was quite alluring. The whole world of hacking was alluring in general. It was a mix of curiosity and fun. But I knew that having this kind of power could have corrupted me. So, I rarely used my hacks, even if they were for good intentions. When I did use them, they were mainly targeted at cyberbullies who liked to pick on weaker people.

The best GunBound matches are between people with equal equipment stats and equal experience. The new players usually don't have much equipment, so their avatars are weaker. The more experienced players usually have better equipment and can easily beat the new players (newbies) without much skill. The bullies are the ones who have the best equipment and purposefully join the games that are full of newbies. The newbies usually are okay with starting the game, because they don't know that they're about to be slaughtered. The bullies have close to a 100% chance of winning the game and gaining the gold coins, while the newbies are left defeated with no gold coins at all. I remember that this happened to me once when I first started playing the game, and it wasn't a pleasant experience.

It was an injustice that I wanted to make right. So what I did was create a new account with no equipment at all. I would then join these games where an entire side would be full of unknowing newbies and the other side would be full of decked out bullies. I didn't do any hacks until the match was almost over, and until the bullies thought that they got another easy win. Just when the newbies started running away after realizing that they were being slaughtered like defenseless lamb, I turned on my hacks. I changed the wind and gravity physics so that during each turn, the bullies would end up shooting themselves. I, then, shot enough lightning bolts at the bullies so that their tank would not get destroyed, but it would end up being buried six feet underground. At that point, they had no place to run to, and they had no chance of shooting any one of the newbies. Their only choices were to quit the game and forfeit, or to shoot at a wall and kill themselves from the blast. The bullies had been defeated either way. Once my anti-bullying tactics became known throughout the GunBound community, there was less and less cyberbullying in the game.

My First Business Venture

Since the price of college books and tuition was high, I had to do what every other college student had to do: Make money on the side. And since GunBound was taking up a lot of my free time, I wanted to find a way to profit from it.

What I had been seeing were people selling their GunBound equipment online for real money. And we're only talking about a few dollars or so for an item that would take hours of playing to obtain. It was a great bargain for players who wanted the powerful items without having to play the game for hours on end. And it was good for people who played the game and wanted to make money on the side. This business model became popular when the online PC game Diablo® came out. People were selling their rare items for tens of dollars on online auction sites.

I realized that I could do pretty well in this business model because I had the advantage of my computer skills. So what I had done was create a hack that made me automatically win after a round begins. I cloned the game and modified it a bit so that it would allow me to run the game more than once on the same computer. This allowed me to play on two accounts in the same computer. Then I coded a computer script that automated the process of starting a new game against my second account. So each time the match started, my primary account would win and get gold for the win. This process, which I nicknamed "gold hack", proved successful, and I was able to generate large amounts of gold even when I was not on my computer (whether I was sleeping or in class). I then used the gold to buy powerful items, which I then sold for real money. I also gave my best friend and some of my other friends all of the most powerful items in the game for free. Being my friend had its benefits.

I also realized that if I sold my gold hack, I would be able to make even more money. So I set the price at $10, and sold hundreds of dollars worth of hacks each day under my blonde hacker girl alias, Janette. This went on for months, and I accumulated enough profits to pay for my college books and my college tuition.

I even became legendary among the GunBound community under my alias. When I was playing, there were people in the game claiming to be or personally know my fictitious hacker alias. The most bizarre incident of this was when my friend from high school, Jason, said that his college classmate, George, claimed to be dating Janette. At the time, none of my friends (or anyone in the world for that matter) knew that I was the one who was pulling the strings behind Janette. So I played a prank on Jason's classmate. I added a new blog post on Janette's blog that said that she dumped George, because it turned out that he had a small penis and cried like a little pansy all the time. I then told Jason to look at Janette's blog, and he cracked up after seeing that post. I later revealed that I personally knew who Janette was and that I spoke to her personally. That decision to reveal my relations to her later bit me in the ass.

Lifehack #16: Your privacy is one of your most important assets.

The invention of the internet only made gossip and rumor spread faster and wider. Word about my relations to Janette traveled pretty quickly and reached many of my friends, even though I told Jason not to tell anyone. Soon, a lot of people from my high school who played GunBound found out that I was actually Janette. The people from my high school were pretty smart, so it wasn't that hard to realize that I was only using her as a cover. After that, it was only a matter of time before word broke out of the circle of friends and onto the internet forums.

Finally, on one fateful day, it happened. I found out about it when my mother called me from New York at one in the morning. I was still in my college dorm in California at the time, so my 1 A.M. was her 4 A.M. What had happened was that a person with a deep-sounding voice had called my mother at four in the morning while pretending to be a police officer. He threatened to arrest me if I didn't stop what I was doing (selling hacks and game items). Soon after she hung up, a different person called her and asked for me. She told him that I wasn't living there anymore and hung up. It was only a few seconds later that she'd receive yet another call. My mother had no idea what I had been up to or what this was all about, so she got scared and confused and called me. Her phone kept getting so many phone calls that almost every time she picked up the phone to try to call me, she'd end up unknowingly answering another phone call. When she finally got through to me, I told her over the phone that

I'd stop my business immediately without really explaining what my business was. I also told her to unplug the phone lines and not to worry.

I immediately went on the GunBound community forums to find out what was going on. What happened was that someone had posted my parents' landline phone number and address on a popular GunBound hacking forum. The address was obtained by doing a reverse phone lookup on my parents' landline phone number. The phone number was obtained through a cached version of one of my old websites. It was a personal website I had made back when I was only 13. It was meant to be a phone directory for my classmates, so that we had a central location to find each others' numbers without having to ask someone else for a person's number. Being 13 meant that I wasn't yet exposed to or lectured on the dangers of revealing your personal information online.

This was a lesson that I'd never forget. The person who posted my parents' number and address thought that it was my number and address. He was not someone I had known, but rather he was a "hacker" who either did not like the idea that I was selling hacks, was a cyberbully, or just wanted to show off his 'doxing' skills. 'Doxing' was the technique used by hackers to gather information about an individual or target using resources obtained through the internet. This information was then assembled to create a target's 'dox' (a word derived from the word 'documents'). The 'dox' was like a hacker's version of a FBI profile on a person. The idea behind it was that when you got a person's 'dox', you knew more about the person, and that increased the likelihood of discovering the person's flaws and vulnerabilities.

For example, there was an infamous case of U.S. vice-presidential candidate Sarah Palin being subjected to hacking. All the hacker needed was Sarah Palin's personal information, such as where she lived and what her pet's name was, to reset her Yahoo email account's password. This allowed that hacker to access all of Sarah Palin's emails.

Nobody was able to hack my accounts, but this person did create a 'dox' on me with all of the personal information that was available online (mainly just my full name, email address, AIM® screen name, home phone number, and home address). Not everyone believed that Janette was a real person. Of those who didn't believe, many wanted to know who was behind that alias. The cover was quite good. It was good enough that people started giving me marriage proposals for being the hottest female hacker. But ultimately, that cover suffered the greatest flaw: my ego. If I had put my ego aside, I would have let Jason's classmate continue his lies and just go on with my business. But once I let that one slip-up occur, things just snowballed forward.

The people on the forums fueled by curiosity, admiration, jealousy, and/or hatred all wanted to call me. The person who had called the number the first time even recorded the conversation with my mother and posted it online. I listened to the frightfulness in my mother's voice, and I couldn't forgive myself for allowing someone to scare my mother like that. I tried burying the forum posts about me by posting random messages on other threads to try to shift the conversation. It eventually worked, but not before the damage had already been done.

I was exposed, and to save my mother from further torment, I had to close my business and lay low. I posted a message on Janette's blog from another hacker alias I made up saying that Janette's accounts have all been hacked, and all the profits from her business were stolen. It was my plan to stop hackers from trying to hack me further. I just wanted them to stop bothering me. But they wouldn't stop. Even my AIM account kept getting messages from hundreds of people as soon as I signed on. Eventually, I had to block everyone who wasn't on my friend list. Two years later, I unblocked everyone, and my AIM account still received many messages asking if I was the infamous Janette. I went back to blocking everyone again since then, and hadn't changed that privacy setting for a very long time.

I was reluctant to close up my business, because I was making thousands of dollars a week from it. But I knew that my family's safety was more important than money. The deranged person who was posing as a police officer had messaged me on AIM and threatened to kill my mother if I didn't stop my business. I felt extremely paranoid at that point, because my father worked long hours, and my fragile mother was alone in the house most of the time. I was also thousands of miles away from home, so I couldn't protect my mother myself. I could have pressed charges at that point for blackmail, but I didn't want to complicate matters more. I was just a college freshman trying to make ends meet and get through college without any trouble.

Although I didn't hand over the matter to the police, I did conduct an investigation of my own to assess the level of threat that this guy posed on my family. That's when I really had to hone my hacking skills. When that person posted an audio file of his conversation with my mother, he posted it up with a unique screen name (it was a variation of "WhiteRabbit"). By searching on that screen name, I found the forums that he frequented and his personal blog. From there, I found out that "WhiteRabbit" was just a young man from Brooklyn who was failing school. But that didn't stop me from still feeling threatened. In his blog, there were pictures of him holding a combat knife. It became obvious that this person was disturbed. His blog also did not supply any personal information about him. There was neither a full name nor a school name on that blog. This was not surprising, because he saw how easily my personal information could be abused online. His paranoia was protecting him. I had to investigate this person even further, and I had to do it fast.

I did not get much information through his blog besides the information about his failing grades and his hatred towards his teachers. I needed a full name, school address and home address in case I ever did need to find him physically. And since I wasn't about to get it through the information found online, I had to set up an elaborate scheme.

The scheme involved creating five websites that were created by different authors and put in different URLs. Each of those authors was a fabricated person, and I was the one behind all of them. One of these fake websites, named "Hackshop", was created by someone trying to sell off his GunBound hacking programs. A second website, created by a hacker named "yyy", was a blog showing off the hacker's hacks ("yyy" was a random hacker alias that I made up). A third website named "HaqBound" was for reviewing and downloading different GunBound hacks for free. A fourth website was a blog post depicting how to buy GunBound items at 10% of its original price. And finally the fifth website was a clone of the official GunBound website.

The first website, "Hackshop", was the website link that I had posted on all the GunBound forums that "WhiteRabbit" frequented. On the forums, I was asking if people knew if this "Hackshop" website was legit or not. I would also then go on another computer and use a different screen name on those forums to reply that the hacks are real and that the website was legit. This was partially true, because I really did set up an e-commerce website to sell the GunBound hacks that I had previously kept to myself (e.g. the unlimited lightning strikes, and gravity/wind modifier). I was able to create the e-commerce website fairly quickly, because I had already coded an e-commerce website when I was selling my GunBound gold hack. It was just a matter of changing the interface so that it wouldn't look like my old shop.

On the "Hackshop" website, I had posted screenshots from a hacker named "yyy" using the available hacks. I also linked to the "yyy" blog using a link titled, "See more screenshots". This was my way of proving that the hacks were real. The users didn't know that both the "yyy" hacker and the owner of "Hackshop" were me. On the "yyy" blog, I talked about how the "Hackshop" website was going against the hacker's ethics of selling hacks for profit. The angered hacker then talked about how he found a hacks-review website called "HaqBound" that had all the hacks sold by "Hackshop" available for free.

On the "HaqBound" website, I created a list of hacks that currently worked and didn't work anymore. I made up some random hacks that didn't work, and I labeled them as "not working". I then labeled some of the hacking programs that I was selling on my "Hackshop" website as "currently working". I also posted a link to download the hacking programs for free. And next to these on the list, was a link to my fourth website, which was a tutorial on how to buy GunBound items at 90% off. I also labeled that hack as "currently working".

On that fourth website, I described how I knew someone who had worked at the company who created GunBound. I explained that GunBound employees had a URL to an employee discount shop that they could give to their friends and families so that they could to buy items at a 90% discount. I explained that the URL was password-protected to prevent abuse, but that I had hacked the password. I posted a link to that URL along with the password that gave them access to the employee discount shop. That link actually redirected users to my clone of the official GunBound website. But back then, there was a bug in the browsers that allowed hackers to mask the URL of the website they were linking to by using some fairly simple

JavaScript commands. So while the link actually pointed to my clone website, the URL shown in the victim's browser was the URL to the official GunBound website.

The clone of the GunBound website was used to "phish" for passwords. As explained earlier, it was a skill that I had learned from people "phishing" on Neopets. What happened was that when people tried to log into the "employee discount shop" using their actual GunBound login information, they would unknowingly email me their username and passwords. And to make the shop look more legit, I edited some actual artwork from the game so that I could use them to decorate the employee discount shop's login page. And to make the shop seem even more legit, I made users enter the employee's password to grant them access to the shop. Obviously this made-up password worked, because I coded the whole cloned website.

After setting up this elaborate bait and trap, all I had to do was hope that WhiteRabbit would see it and fall for it. Each one of the websites I created played a role in convincing WhiteRabbit to enter his username and password. For example, "Hackshop" was a spin-off of the original shop I had to sell my gold hacks. I knew that WhiteRabbit hated these shops for whatever reason that may be. I created this hacker named "yyy" as a person WhiteRabbit could relate to. This hacker also hated "Hackshop" and recommended users go to the "HaqBound" website to get hacks for free. I knew that WhiteRabbit wanted hacks for free, because he frequented a lot of forums that discussed GunBound hacking. The purpose of "yyy" was to build WhiteRabbit's trust in the "HaqBound" website by personally recommending it. By putting working hacks in the "HaqBound" website, I further built WhiteRabbit's trust on the website. Many people started sharing the HaqBound website and saying how good it was. I never personally recommended HaqBound on the forums myself, because I was a new user to the forums, and usually people don't trust links given by new users. That's why I had to make the other established and trusted users on the forums post links to the HaqBound website for me. My plan worked, and soon everyone trusted the HaqBound website. Once I had that trust, it was easy to convince people that an employee discount shop actually existed, and they trusted me enough to follow the tutorial written on another blog. By putting the discount shop tutorial on another blog, I had shifted the blame away from HaqBound. That way, when the more veteran hackers realized that the discount shop was a phishing scam, they wouldn't put the blame on HaqBound. I could not lose people's trust in HaqBound or else WhiteRabbit might not visit the website himself. I also had to defend the reputation of HaqBound on the forums by replying to the whistleblowers who tried to expose the phishing scam. I said that the discount only worked for certain users and that while it worked for my older accounts, it did not work for my new ones. It was just a matter of time before HaqBound got exposed, so I was praying that WhiteRabbit would fall for the trap soon.

Finally, after three weeks, and more than a thousand phished accounts later, I had finally got WhiteRabbit's GunBound username and password. He realized that it was scam and changed his GunBound password immediately. But, it was not his GunBound account that I was after. I immediately used his password on his personal blog. From there I found his personal email address. I used his password on his email account and quickly shifted through his emails until I found his real name, home address and phone number from an invoice he received. I also learned almost everything else about the person, such as which school he went to, and which internet provider he used. I was in and out of that email account before he had the chance to change the password.

So to recap, all I needed was a person's screen name to get all that information. Let that be a lesson to not use a unique screen name online. And try not to use the same screen name across different websites. Your screen name acts as your unique ID through the internet, and people can trace your web history by searching on that screen name on a search engine.

By getting WhiteRabbit's identity, I finally got what I wanted: Reassurance that if this person would do anything bad to my mother, I would know how to find him immediately. Without this reassurance, it was difficult for me to concentrate in class. I was also worried that something had already happened to my mother, and I'd be the one responsible for bringing an evil person to her. My worries didn't go away until months later, when people started forgetting about the matter. I had tried to delete every bit of evidence of my family's existence from the internet. I removed all of my parent's information online, including their home phone number and address.

I removed all my public profiles and personal websites. For about a decade after that incident, I had kept a low profile.

Fortunately, nothing really happened after that. And that's also what's great about the internet. It makes people easily distracted. Once your 15-minutes of fame are up, you quickly become old news. People will move onto other things. The same speed that you rush into stardom is roughly the same speed that you'll rush out of it.

But be warned that if you stand out, there will always be people trying hard to take you down. They will even dedicate a lot of their free time to do so. The reasoning is not always clear as to why they do it. Perhaps they feel that everyone should be equal and that the idea of you being successful threatens that equality. Perhaps they feel that the only people who become successful are the ones who are greedy and obtain wealth through ill-gotten ways. Whatever the reason is, that's just the way life is. That's why you must value your privacy and anonymity immensely. Social networks like Facebook® are taking away your most precious asset. And they are doing it for their own profits. Keep some mystery in your life. Silence your ego, and don't be so quick to announce your fortunes.

For those who are curious as to what happened to WhiteRabbit: A few months after the incident, I felt like I needed to get some revenge for what WhiteRabbit did to my mother. So I took some of my accounts, and sent several GunBound items to WhiteRabbit. Then in each account, I complained to the GunBound employees that someone stole my items. I also took some screenshots of me using hacks and modified them so that it looked like it was

WhiteRabbit's character that was doing the hacking. I then posted the screenshots on my Hackshop website and pretended that I forgot to blur out my account name. I then sent a link to Hackshop to the GunBound employees and complained that a hacker named WhiteRabbit was cheating in the game. The GunBound employees ultimately flagged WhiteRabbit as a hacker and banned his GunBound account.

Lifehack #17: Don't conduct businesses that won't allow you to sleep well at night.

The entire GunBound business gave me confidence that even an 18-year-old could harness the technology of the internet to become successful. What was also great was that building a website cost only a few dollars. And in some cases, it cost nothing at all. Back then, if you wanted to start a successful business, you had to invest in commercial real estate or rent a store or buy some products first before you could sell them. This new business model of low investment and high returns was what I aimed for. And it was a successful business model that I could apply over and over again to many products.

The GunBound community was small (users in the thousands) compared to the World of Warcraft® community (users in the millions). For those who don't know, World of Warcraft is a massively multiplayer online role-playing game (MMORPG), where you choose a hero and do things with the hero to get gold to buy better equipment or to level up. I figured that if I could create hacks for World of Warcraft instead, I would make way more than what I made when I was selling hacks for GunBound.

And that became a reality for at least one person. Another hacker/programmer had created a program that would play the game for you, so that you wouldn't have to do the repetitive and tedious task of killing creatures to earn gold and experience. This program was known to hackers as a 'bot' (which is short for 'robot'). He made a lot of money in a short amount of time by selling that bot for about $25 each. He sold over a hundred thousand copies of them, because a lot of people did not really have the free time to play through the game for hours upon hours to get to the level that they wanted. It was also worth it because you could take the gold you earned from running the bot and sell the gold for real money. This was what a lot of so-called "Chinese farmers" would do. Chinese companies would pay young people in China a few cents an hour to play World of Warcraft and gather gold for them. Those companies would then sell the gold for real money in the black market. This whole underworld economy of online-hacking and MMORPG e-commerce spelled for big money.

I could have easily gotten into this business. I had written powerful hacks and programs for the game. I wrote a program that would play the game for me as well, and it would help me collect the gold. The great thing was that I wrote the program myself, so it was not detectable by the World of Warcraft game client. The other programmer had the issue of constantly updating his program to keep it working. The company behind World of Warcraft would keep detecting the program and updating its game so that the bot would stop working. This back and forth went on for years until the company finally decided to sue the creator of the bot for violating its copyrights and trademarks. His bot sales ceased, and he was stuck paying the lawyer fees.

There was another story about how another young hacker had made about a million dollars a month selling his hacks. He bought two Lamborghini®'s (a Twin Turbo Gallardo® and a Murcielago®), but he, too, got shut down, and his high income was suddenly cut off. The sad thing was that he blew through most of his most money by throwing expensive parties and buying depreciating assets, such as his exotic cars. And this is a pitfall for someone who makes a lot of money in a short period of time. They think their high income will last forever, so they start spending money they haven't made yet.

The problem with selling shady products is that you'd never know when you will get shut down, sued, or arrested. If I had sold my World of Warcraft hacks, I could have been in the same legal trouble that the other bot creator was in. I knew how much trouble I got from selling my GunBound hacks, and it deterred me from repeating the same mistakes. I remembered how many nights I had trouble sleeping because I didn't know what kind of bad news I'd get the next day. I was even conditioned to be afraid of the new email alert sound. Every new email I got could have contained bad news.

This was not a risk worth taking, even if it'd make me millions of dollars. I would never go into a business where I wouldn't know whether I'd still be free from jail the next day. Just the paranoia alone would have eaten me up. And if the business only caused me to get sued, then it would have devastated me to suddenly lose all of my income. The feeling of losing millions of dollars in a few days would be brutal. It was the kind of drop in income that caused many celebrities to turn to drugs after they failed to make another hit movie or another hit song.

That's why I never sold my World of Warcraft hacks. I kept them for myself only. It was tempting to head back down that road where I'd continue selling hacks and making thousands of dollars. But having a clear conscience and the ability to sleep well at night was worth more than money could buy.

Even in the present, the opportunity to run shady businesses with high income still rears its head every once in a while. I still do not think it is worth it and always turn those offers down. I've seen many young people take this route of easy money. Some of them get away with it, but most of them don't stop until they've gotten burned. Sometimes being burned doesn't equate to just financial losses. Sometimes their reputation gets smeared as well, and people start losing their trust in them. And since it's hard to erase something from the internet, the damages last for quite awhile once your reputation gets ruined.

10 CAREER PATH

While I technically started web development in my early teens, I never got paid for my work until my late teens. Web development was great, because it combined several skill sets that I wanted to develop. It was a mix of graphics design, coding, and marketing.

My graphics design skills were a natural talent of mine. Since I was very young, I could draw things in small details with accuracy. It could have been a talent passed on by my father, because he was an excellent artist as well. As I looked at more artwork from other artists, I got a better understanding of what was considered beautiful and what was not. Once you had the eye for that, then graphics design became easier.

My coding skills were a natural progression from my skills with logic and creative thinking. Those two skills were the reason why I kept scoring in the 99 percentile for national math exams. It was my lack of great memory and my small vocabulary that hampered my overall exam scores and prevented me from attending the top schools. Luckily, the ability to code relied more on logic and creative thinking than on memory. And that's how I naturally progressed into being a programmer. It was a very effective use of my talents and my weaknesses did not hinder my progression in the field.

My marketing skills came from a mix of my experiences and my ability to sympathize with others. By always putting myself in the customer's shoes, I gained a better perspective on how to market my products better. And through experience, I could tell which marketing techniques worked and which did not.

Through these skill sets, I was able to land a job at my college as a webmaster. I also was paid to code websites for other companies and even for a fraternity once (ZBT). While I had already known HTML, CSS, and JavaScript from developing websites as a teenager, I had to learn how to code in PHP and SQL on my own.

I remembered that when I first interviewed for the job of webmaster at my college, I admitted that I did not know PHP and SQL (skills that they were looking for). I showed them my portfolio of websites done in Flash and JavaScript, and they were impressed enough to give me a chance. I basically had a few weeks to learn enough PHP and SQL to create an entire chemistry department website. So, I used my free time to quickly pick up PHP and SQL. To this day, I've never taken a formal class on PHP. And yet, when I took a proficiency test at a head hunting firm, I passed the PHP test with flying colors. This pretty much gave me the confidence to believe that if I were given enough time and educational resources, I could learn and develop in any computer language in a short period of time without ever going to school for it. This confidence later gave me the motivation to learn Objective-C and to create apps when few people knew how to create apps.

But I didn't jump into making apps at the beginning of my career. I went the safe route first and got myself a stable job. I was being realistic with myself, because I knew that success will not be achieved by everyone. I had to make sure that there was a safety net under me first before I took the leap of faith.

Lifehack #18: Have a contingency plan.

Some people get stuck on the idea that they're really good at something when they're only mediocre at best. They've lied to themselves (or they've been lied to) so many times about how good their talents are, that they start thinking that they can lead a successful career from it.

I would then see the same person spend years trying to book gigs for their talent and only make a few hundreds of dollars here and there. It was not nearly enough for a career, and they were only making ends meet. But they still go at it, because they do not know what else to do at that point. They did not discover what their other talents were and did not have another skill set to fall back on. When I started coding apps, I still had my web development skills to fall back on in case my app coding was not that great. These people did not have a back-up career, and now they're practically living in poverty and begging for money (in forms of gigs).

These people end up being a drag on the family members who support them. Not only are they in a financial mess, they will most likely lose all confidence in themselves and have suicidal tendencies. And if they have children, then it only makes matters worse, because they are also responsible for providing for their children.

That is why it is always important to have a contingency plan in case your ambitions fail. That way, you can have the confidence you need to continue your ambitions without the fear of becoming broke. Even if you have a "never give up" attitude when it comes to your ambition, it is still good to acknowledge that there's a possibility that your plans could fail.

When I started making large amounts of money from apps, I did not quit my day job right away. My day job was my contingency plan, and it helped remove my fears that if my apps would stop selling one day, then I'd become broke. It was after I made my second million dollars from my apps that I decided to quit my job. I had saved up enough money to last me for several years, and I would have been okay even if I lost all my income and could not get a job right away. That was the only time I was willing to let my contingency plan go.

However, even after I've made enough money for a lifetime, I am still exploring my talents to see what else I am good at. They're more like hobbies, and I don't actually expect to become wealthy from them. For example, I have recently taken up acting, photography, and even book writing. This very book is a part of my exploration of my talents. And because of my wealth, I am able to use these high-risk careers as my new contingency plan. Those who cannot afford this luxury should look for more stable careers as their contingency plans. And if you have a diploma from college, then you can use that when trying to land that back-up job.

Once you have that part of your life settled, it's time to explore your talents and use those talents to launch your successful business.

Lifehack #19: Figure out what you love and what you're good at.

I have a friend named Ariana who knows little about coding, but is amazing at photography and graphics design. Those who are in the photography business know that it's very hard to get wealthy from being a photographer. So what she did was create a blog about her photography tips, and she made money through the ads on that blog. Sometimes, she would post Amazon affiliate links to the camera products that she used and gain commission for the sales that she helped make through her blog.

Later on, she became even more successful when she started selling Photoshop templates to photographers. The templates basically allow photographers to easily insert their pictures into a photo of a living room wall. This allowed photographers to show their clients how their pictures would look on their living room wall if they bought prints from them. It also helped the clients understand how their pictures would look in different sizes on the wall. She makes about $15,000 a month from selling these templates. And now, she has released an iPad® app called "Shoot and Sell" that does the same thing.

It goes to show that you don't really need to be a great coder to create websites and apps. You don't need to be the most talented person in the world. And you don't need to be talented in everything. All you have to do is find out what you're good at by learning as many different things as time will allow you. When you finally stumble upon a talent that you have a natural skill for, you should keep practicing that talent until you get really good at it. And to tell if you're good at what you're doing, you'll have to see if people are willing to pay you for your talents. If they are, then you've discovered your main marketable skill set. If not, then you should just think of it as a hobby and move on with your life.

When you're trying to discover your marketable talents, try to find something that you love doing. Sometimes loving what you do in life is what keeps you going when the going gets tough. Sometimes you just need to find something you used to do as a child, and expand on that. I loved computers when I was a child, and I made a business out of it. If you look at every successful person, you can almost always trace back their talents to something they did when they were younger. Whether they sang when they were younger or played golf when they were younger, they all shared the common success story of doing something that they had a passion for since they were young.

"Sometimes life hits you in the head with a brick. Don't lose faith. I'm convinced that the only thing that kept me going was that I loved what I did. You've got to find what you love. And that is as true for your work as it is for your lovers. Your work is going to fill a large part of your life, and the only way to be truly satisfied is to do what you believe is great work."

– Steve Jobs

11 RETAIL BUSINESS

Besides web development, I enjoyed fixing other people's computers. When I was just a teenager, I used to fix my neighbors' computers for free. I even held a job at Best Buy's Geek Squad once during college. And since my job required me to interact with the customers, I picked up a few retail business lessons while working there.

The job was not all about fixing people's computers. I was also a salesman and a customer service representative at the same time. At the job, they taught me to push the computer owners to upgrade their computer while I was servicing their computer. They told me that once I got my foot through the door, I had a great opportunity to make some sales. It was from that tip that I learned to advertise other apps on my apps.

They also taught me about the different types of customers that existed in the retail ecosystem. There were the ones who had a lot of money, but not a lot of time. Those were the ones who you could push value-added services onto. They would be more willing to pay for installation setups and premium features such as expensive cables and more powerful video cards. They wanted the best, and money wasn't an issue for them. Then on the opposite side of the spectrum, there were people who wanted the most value for their money. They wanted to squeeze everything they could out of their penny. These are the ones who you had to explain in detail why they must upgrade and why they need something. And these are the ones who would jump on any chances of a sale.

The way to deal with the customers changes dramatically depending on who you are dealing with. And knowing how to appeal to both sides of the spectrum (and everyone in between) is the best way to maximize your profits.

App development tip #3: Tailor to different types of customers.

One of the most asked questions about app development is how much you should charge for an app and whether or not to create a free version of your app. The answer is that you should sell your app to both the rich and the frugal. If you charge too much for your app, then you only get sales from the ones who have that kind of money to fling around. If you charge too little for an app, then you might be losing out on some chances to maximize your profits. For example, if your app is $1 instead of $2, then your app sales better be more than double the app sales of when you sold your app for $2. In some cases, charging $2 actually increases your profits even more. But you also lose the sale to those who would have been willing to pay only

$1 for the app. So what can you try doing? Sell your app for $1, but sell additional features as an in-app purchase. That way you get the people who are willing to pay $1. And you also can get profits from those who have extra money through your in-app purchases.

If you go even one step further, you can also create a free app. Apple allows you to sell both a free version of your app and a paid version. So take advantage of that fact and create a free version of your app to get profits from those who aren't even willing to pay a dollar for your app. Just put a banner ad in that free version and remove some of the extra features.

The great thing about having an ad-driven free app is that even if your paid app loses popularity in the future, you will still get consistent ad revenue from those who already downloaded your app and will still be using it. I have had to deal with the issue of my 5-0 Radio app losing steam after being in the top of the App Store for over three years. With more competitors nibbling away at my sales and the fact that I'm running out of interested customers to sell to, it was inevitable for 5-0 Radio to drop in sales gradually. However, the ad revenue gained by the free version of 5-0 Radio has been growing steadily. At the time of this writing, my ad revenue has surpassed my paid app revenue by two-three folds. And if you combine both my paid apps revenue and my free apps revenue, my overall revenue has been growing steadily each year.

App development tip #4: Grow your user base.

The other major benefit of having a free app is the ability to grow your user base by over ten folds. As a rule of thumb, free app downloads are almost always ten times more than your paid app downloads (if popularity remains the same and your paid app only costs a dollar). And having a large user base is very powerful, especially when combined with social media.

If you're aware of how viral marketing works, then you'll understand the benefits of word-of-mouth marketing. I've made it a personal commitment to never buy advertisements for my apps. I've been relying heavily on word-of-mouth marketing, and in this day and age of social media, word-of-mouth marketing has never been easier.

Create a Facebook page for your app, and add a "like" button in your app for your Facebook page. This is free advertisement for your app. Your users are advertising your app to their friends each time they "like" your Facebook page. Take it one step further and add Facebook integration to your app. Have your app have the option to post "achievements" on your users' timeline (for example, have your app post a top game score on their timeline). Some users like to brag about their achievements, so they will be the ones willing to post these achievements. What they may not be aware of is that they're helping you advertise your app without you paying them. If you want to be even more extreme, you can integrate Twitter®, and other social media websites to further your exposure.

Keep in mind that there is no greater advertisement for your app than when someone, who a potential customer trusts, recommends your app. Therefore, when those potential customers see those Facebook status updates or Twitter tweets about your app, they are more willing to download your app than if they saw your app rotated into some ad banner. That is why having a large user base is important, even if you lose some paid app sales to your free version. The user may have gotten the app for free, but you potentially gained a free salesman. And those friends of the user who got the app in turn will help advertise your app even further. That's the basis for viral marketing.

Thus, growing your user base is same as growing your army of salesmen. And if you create other products, you can also sell those products to your user base as well to further harness the power of having a large user base. That's why the popular app Angry Birds® now has Halloween costumes, stuffed dolls, t-shirts, and other merchandise. Not only are they getting revenue for their merchandise, they are also creating walking human advertisements for their products.

App development tip #5: Learn how to interact with your users.

Besides turning your users into salesmen, you can also turn them into your quality control manager and your boss. Keep in mind that the success of an app is almost never about luck. Apps have to click with the users. The litmus test is to see if even you will use the app yourself. That is the test I do whenever I code a new app. If I am not using the app myself, then I think it is a failure. At that point, I'd either scrap the idea or keep improving the app until it got to the point where I liked using it.

That is why it is important to listen to user feedback and implement the changes that they want. Chances are that if at least one or two users have a complaint about the app, then there are hundreds and maybe even thousands of other people who have the same complaint. Those other ones who haven't been vocal about their complaints either live with it, or do not want to spend their free time complaining about it.

Always address the negative feedback that you receive. Do not take constructive criticism personally. Instead, try to fix your bugs and add the features that users are requesting. If your app's reviews are not constantly averaging with 4.5 stars or higher, then you need to either fix your app or come up with a new app.

A friend of mine who's also an app developer used to ignore his negative feedback. His ego made him block out the criticism. He thought his app was one of the best apps ever made, and thus, he labeled all of his negative critics as haters. Every time he got a negative review, he was in denial and said that the review must have come from a competitor or a hater. His app was actually pretty good, but his sales were hurting because of the negative reviews he received. He asked me for help, so I played around with his app and told him what needed to be changed in the app to make it better. A lot of the changes that I thought could have helped the app were actually similar to the complaints made by his "haters". He finally listened and made the changes to his app. Since then, his app's reviews have been mostly positive, and his sales have been growing because of the positive reviews.

Thus, don't do what my friend did in the beginning. Instead, do the complete opposite. When you get emails with complaints and feature-requests, thank the senders and tell them that you are getting on it immediately. This usually stalls them from leaving your app a bad review, if they haven't left one for your app already. When they see the changes, they will praise your app, because these users are not used to being heard by big companies. They are used to getting the same politically-correct, cookie-cutter response from some outsourced customer service representative. This happens usually when they send an email to a large American corporation. By personalizing your emails and reassuring them that their complaints are heard from the makers of the app, you are developing a potentially rewarding mutual bond with them. They get the changes they want, and you get a satisfied customer who will praise your app to other people.

Users love when their voices are heard, and love it even more when they are individually responsible for actual changes to products. A lot of my positive reviews in the early days have been from customers who praised me for having great customer service. I was quick and responsive in my interactions with them. Whenever there was a change requested, I emailed them back within the hour, and told them that I would make the change immediately or in the next version. Then, I would actually spend the time implementing the changes and pushing the change out to the App Store as soon as possible. This went back and forth for many versions of my apps (with at least 20 versions for 5-0 radio alone). Finally, my apps stopped receiving complaints and feature requests, because they had nothing left to complain about. And now my apps are constantly getting overwhelmingly more positive reviews than negative reviews. And as those who have ever done online shopping would know, positive reviews for a product are extremely important when people decide whether or not to get your product.

Besides making changes based on user feedback, you should use the app everyday and implement the changes that you would like to see yourself. By making an app that people want to use, the app promotes and markets itself, because users will tell their friends and family to download the app. Thus, customer interaction is important and is something you should invest your time in.

Lifehack #20: Treat customers like they're the only ones left in the world.

Sometimes we can be dismissive of people if we feel that they are a waste of our time. We may get impatient with how slow someone is to understanding what you are saying. We may get frustrated with how ignorant someone can be. We may get offended by how inappropriate a person is being. We're very tempted to just walk away from these people or even give them an earful. But in the world of business, you must treat each customer like he/she was the only customer you will ever have.

It does not matter who you're speaking to. You must not judge them based on their looks, age, financial status, or gender. You may think that pandering to only the wealthy would get you further in profits. But then you'd be forgetting the power of social media. You know that waitress working for minimal wage down at the local diner? She has thousands of friends on Facebook. You know that rich housewife who's eating at the local diner? She only has a few dozen friends. If you get that waitress hooked on your product, you're potentially spreading the word about your product to thousands of people. If you get that wealthy housewife hooked on the app, then you're probably only spreading the word to a few of her country club friends.

So, don't be dismissive of a person who you think is not going to be a great customer. That customer could be your greatest salesman or your greatest reviewer. When I first walked into one of the Lamborghini dealerships in sneakers and a pair of jeans, I got dismissed by the sales representatives working there – my age might have had something to do with it as well. They thought that I'm just another teenager trying to get a free exotic car show. That kind of dismissive attitude left a bad taste in my mouth, and I ultimately never bought a Lamborghini from them. Now that I've bought my second new Lamborghini already from another dealership, they're inviting me to car unveilings and private parties. As a customer, I felt that the relationship was already broken the day they were dismissive of me. It goes to show you that you can't really judge a customer by how they look.

Even your next door neighbor could be a millionaire, and you would never know it by the car he drives or the clothes he wears. Looks can be quite deceiving, and frankly, I would be suspicious of someone who feels the need to show off his wealth. The millionaires who can stay humble and low-key are the ones who gain the most respect from me. And since these low-key millionaires are incognito, I always treat every customer of mine like he is a personal friend. You can only do right when you treat people with respect and care. When a customer feels good about doing business with you, they sometimes are willing to pay higher prices just for the better customer service.

12 GRADUATING

After I graduated from college, I started my career in Pasadena, CA at EarthLink®, an internet service provider. It was your typical nine-to-five office cubicle job that every college graduate went to school for. The pay was competitive for an entry-level college graduate and the environment was casual enough that I didn't feel stressed out. I recall the days when my colleagues and I started a Starcraft® LAN party during one of the moving days (they had moved to a new office building during my stay there). And when there was massive restructuring of the company (where some people lost their jobs and some had to move to another branch), I threw a Wii® party for everyone. We used one of the projectors and one of the conference rooms to play Wii games on a 12-foot wall. It was more of a going-away party, but we labeled that meeting as "user interface research".

What's interesting about EarthLink was that it had very bright-minded engineers and programmers, but the company was too slow to adapt. The massive layoffs wouldn't have happened if they weren't losing massive revenue each year. The problem was that they relied on their dial-up service too much, and never really expanded quickly enough to other services. It was the same fate that AOL suffered with their ISP branch. While other companies quickly adopted broadband technology over dial-up services, EarthLink was a bit too slow to jump the gun. They eventually woke up around the time that I arrived, and downsized their company to focus more on new technology and core services. And it was sad to see the downsizing happen, because that company lost a lot of veteran programmers and engineers who have been there for over a decade. There was even one guy there who graduated from U.C. Berkeley in his teens.

Nonetheless, I was ready to take on the world and to begin my career like everyone else was doing. I had side jobs such as fixing computers, developing websites and selling World of Warcraft items that I obtained through my programs. But, most of them were really just hobbies rather than actual successful businesses. I wasn't so worried about making money at that point. I was just happy to have a great job and not have to worry about being unemployed after graduation.

The Phone Call

That all changed with a single phone call.

It is late at night at the apartment that I am staying at in California. It hasn't even been four months since I graduated from college. It is my aunt on the other line. We speak in Chinese.

"Hi, Allen. How are you? I'm your aunt. Do you remember me?" She asks in a calm voice.

"Oh, hi, Auntie," I respond back while half awake. "How are you?"

She says, "Do you know that your father passed away today? What are you going to do? You have to pick up your father's body. I already told your brother about it. But I can't get a hold of your mother." It is two in the morning in New York. My mother is probably sound asleep.

"Wait, what?" I ask in disbelief. "My dad is dead? How? Why?"

"I don't know all the details yet, but the hospital confirmed that he's dead," she responds. She now seems to be in a rush to get off the phone. I suspect that she was hoping that she wouldn't be the one who'd have to break the news to me. "Call your mother when you can and book a flight to China as soon as possible. If you need someone to talk to, feel free to call me, okay?"

She hangs up.

That was the end of the worst phone call I had ever received.

Burned Into Memory

At that point, my entire immediate family was spread across the globe. My mother was in New York City. My brother was in London, after graduating from Imperial College with a Ph.D. My father was in China visiting his older sister. I was in California. We had a running joke in the family that the Sun never set on our family. It took my father's death to finally bring us all together again for the first time in several years.

When we got to China, we headed for the morgue to find my father. I went in there with my mother to ID the body. She grabbed my hand really tightly when the coroner pulled the sheets back to reveal a naked body. She had a sliver of hope when we arrived there. She hoped that it wasn't him and that it was all a mistake. That hope went out the window when we saw his face.

It was a surreal moment to see my father's cold, motionless body in the morgue. His face was placed on top of what was left of his cracked skull like a Halloween mask. It was definitely him. There was no denying it. It was one of those images that were so disturbing that they burned into your memory. I could recall that image very clearly even years later.

The cause of his death is not something I wish to repeat. Those who caused his death were never punished. They have probably moved on now, and no longer feel guilty. Justice has failed my father.

However, I do not wish to go into further details on this matter. I've learned to forgive those responsible and to move on with my life. Dwelling in the past prevents you from moving forward, and stops you from leading a healthy and happy life.

"Do not pray for an easy life, pray for the strength to endure a difficult one"

– Bruce Lee

13 AFTERMATH

The next few months that followed were the most grueling months I had to face. My father left us some inheritance money, but it wasn't enough to last us forever. Most of our inheritance was tied in real estate and mutual funds, and we couldn't access the money until we sold those assets. Unfortunately for us, he passed away at the beginning of the Great Recession of 2008. So, the value of the real estate and stocks he left us tanked and still has not recovered years later.

To make matters worse, my father's sudden and unnatural death caused my mother to start having mental problems. So, I moved back into my mother's house in New York to take care of her. This move across the country ended my relationship with my college girlfriend of over two years. It also meant that I had to look for a new job in New York.

My brother, on the other hand, stayed in London to continue being with his college girlfriend of over four years (they eventually got married in 2012). She had to stay in London, because she was enrolled in medical school there. The only problem was that during the global recession, nobody was looking to hire an entry-level Ph.D. graduate. Since companies had to cut back on their budget, they rather hire B.S. graduates and train them themselves.

My mother, who was a homemaker, was too devastated and mentally unsound to hold a job. This meant that for months after my father's death, nobody in our family had a steady income, and we were only living off of our savings.

The mental as well as fiscal blow to our family would have crushed most families. These were adversities that we wouldn't even wish upon our enemies. But none of us gave up. We were down, but not defeated yet.

Columbia University

It was not until I landed a job at a research facility in Columbia University that our family started having an income again. At the job, I helped with web development and helped marine biologists with organizing and displaying their data using computer programs. Together, we studied the deep sea and analyzed the effects of climate change. We also looked to discover new deep sea species, and to figure out new ways to combat the growing concentration of greenhouse gasses in our atmosphere.

The salary was not very competitive. I was getting paid only slightly more than what the average American was making. But I took the job over my other higher-salary job offers, because it fitted more with my ideals of making this world a better place. Whether or not people believed in global warming didn't matter much. There was no denying that there is a higher concentration of greenhouse gasses in the atmosphere now compared to decades ago because of our growing livestock, melting ice caps, deforestations, and burning of fossil fuels. Studying the effects of that was vital for the future of this planet.

Lifehack #21: Don't wait around. Create your own opportunities.

This was around the time when the App Store started accepting new apps. I was very intrigued with the idea of having your phone do whatever you wanted it to do. It seemed like something out of a science fiction movie, and the possibilities for innovations were endless. It seemed like a great opportunity for me to do great things, and that's what I needed in a life where everything else dragged me down. Rather than waiting and watching other people take advantage of the opportunity, I seized the opportunity when it presented itself.

At my job in Columbia University, I asked my employers if they could give me a MacBook® as my work computer. You needed an Apple computer to code and submit apps at the time, and I wasn't rich enough to just drop $1,100 on a new MacBook. As soon as I got my MacBook, I learned how to code in Objective-C on my own by reading books and playing with the code. Ever since I was young, I had a fascination with learning new skills and using those skills to help people or to create things that helped people.

My father was the same way. And he was the one who taught me to persevere during stressful times, and to take my education into my own hands. His passing was unexpected, and it pushed me out of my comfort zone. But before his passing, he had already left me the tools I needed to take on the responsibilities that ensued.

Since I was the only one making money at the time, I had to step up as the breadwinner for the family, despite being only 22. So I knew that I had to work on more profitable side projects during the times when I wasn't working at my full-time job (i.e. nights and weekends). Thus, coding apps during my free time made sense to me. While my peers were slowly eased into adulthood, I was pushed into the deep end of the pool without warning. I went from being a dependent to an independent to an independent with dependents within the span of a few months. So, his passing fast-forwarded my life, and the burden, responsibilities and stress I received strengthened my character.

But I wasn't always that strong. I admit that I had contemplated suicide during the days when life became too unbearable (because of my father's death, mother's mental illness, and stress from holding two jobs and a social life). But I could never go through with it. I had too many responsibilities and too many people relying on me to let them down. Suicide was a coward's way out. I had only fantasized about it. Even just being in a temporary fantasy of nothingness made my life of misery a bit more bearable.

For those thinking about suicide, please realize that it is a stupid way out. As with stocks and roller coasters, when you are at the lowest point in your life, you are only giving yourself more room to go upwards. Why leave this world at the lowest point of your life? You're going to miss out on all the wonderful things that have yet to come.

"When written in Chinese the word crisis is composed of two characters. One represents danger, and the other represents opportunity."

– John F. Kennedy

This would have been a great motivational meme if it were true. But the truth is that the second character in the word crisis only partially means opportunity. The second character can mean other things as well. In fact, the second character in crisis has a closer meaning to "crucial point" than it does to "opportunity." Thus to avoid spreading this false meme further, I will use a less eloquent quote from an unlikely philosopher:

"To hell with circumstances; I create opportunities."

– Bruce Lee

14 AGE OF THE APPS

Some may think that it was pure luck that I made millions from apps. I don't blame those people for thinking that way. It's an easy-to-swallow way of comprehending the situation. But, luck had very little to do with it. Luck is when you win a lottery ticket. Making an app that has over a million dollars in profits per year? As you'll find out, it takes a whole lot more than just luck.

> "God doesn't play dice with the world"
>
> – Albert Einstein

My very first app was a browser. It was a great starting point, because everyone wants a good browser. You almost always want to create a product that has mass appeal. I wasn't satisfied with Safari's lack of the ability to hide its toolbars or lack of a privacy setting (which they added later), so I decided to create my own browser. The browser wasn't a million dollar success, but it was well received enough to stay in the Top 50 charts in the Utilities section. Back then, that meant that it earned about $50 per day.

It was sort of a gold rush in the beginning if $50 per day can be called a gold rush. It was also a gold rush in the sense that there was not much competition at the time. The big companies had not yet stepped in during the first year, so you were mainly competing against other independent developers. Since I knew how to do graphics design, web development, user-interface creation, programming, and marketing, I was basically my own company. Most developers were either great at coding or great at graphics design. But rarely were they great at both. And for those who were great at both, it was even rarer for them to know how to market their apps. Thus, I had an advantage over the rest because I could do all of those things. Nowadays, apps are created by a team of people, and you will rarely find apps created by just one person in the top charts.

In the beginning, the biggest challenge was that there weren't many iPhone developers at the time, so you pretty much had to learn everything on your own without the help of anyone. Nowadays, you can just search on the internet for your programming question, and there will probably be a dozen developers who would have posted an answer to your question already.

The other big challenge was that your app could be cloned easily, since the app wasn't complex enough. It wasn't long before other browser alternatives started to pop up. I had to innovate to keep my browser on the top charts. One of the innovations was the ability to hide ad banners as you browsed the web. So I implemented ad-blocking technology into my browser app. I also wanted to make the browser have cool features that an iPhone could do, but a laptop or desktop computer couldn't. So, I invented a way to scroll through websites by just tilting the phone. The more you tilted, the faster it scrolled.

App development tip #6: Have features worthy of showing off.

The ad-blocking and tilt-scrolling features were good enough to amaze the people I showed it to. Those features were what I'd call 'hooks'. Usually, every popular app has a hook to it. Instagram® got popular because of its ability to turn your pictures into vintage-looking pictures. Pandora® got popular because of its ability to stream popular music for free. Those were what hooked people onto the app.

In addition, those hooks also act as bait for new customers. As I mentioned before, the best marketing you can get is from word-of-mouth. Meaning that if you have a feature that's worthy of showing off to your friends, then it's very likely that your current customers will show off the app to their friends. Then, their friends will want the app as well and download it.

People like to follow trends and don't want to be the only ones without something. In the animal world, you see this behavior in groups of the same species. Similar birds tend to flock together and fly in the same direction. Schools of fish tend to travel long distances together in the same direction as well. Studies have shown they behave this way instinctually. These animals follow one another, because the ones that stray away from the group tend to end up as food for predators. The ones that stayed in a group have a higher survival rate and thus, are more likely to pass on their genes. The ones that strayed from the group have a lower survival rate (as well as a lower chance of finding a mate), so they are less likely to pass on their genes. If you keep up this trend for millions of years, then the only animals left alive are the ones who flock together.

People are very similarly behaved. If you look at clothing, it is not hard to see that a lot of people dress alike. And if you look at houses and cars, you would not see much variety either. The only ones who look different are the leaders and the independent thinkers. There are much fewer people of this type than there are people who just follow what other people do. And it's not always a conscious choice being made. Some of the behavior is done subconsciously and can even be predicted. For example, there was a psychology experiment done involving a few people inside an elevator that opened from the front or the back. A majority of the people on the elevator was aware of the test and knew exactly which of the two doors was going to open when the elevator stopped. What they did was turn away from the door that was going to open next and faced the wrong door. The majority of the time, the person or persons who aren't in on the experiment would follow the crowd and turn away from the correct door as well. It may not happen right away, but they don't want to look like the odd person out. So, they eventually turn around. And if the majority of the group then turns back the correct way, the same people who were following also turns around again.

This behavior is not abnormal. Instead, our instinct to group together and work together to create a community has been passed on for millions of years. That is why it is more important to create features that set the trend, rather than create features that follow a trend. There are many clones of Instagram, and some are genuinely better photo editors than Instagram. But since Instagram popularized the whole vintage photo-editing feature, they've been staying on the top for quite a while.

This doesn't mean that you have to be first ones to do it. Instagram actually copied that feature from other apps that had the same feature for months. Even Instagram itself wasn't popular until months after their first release. But the first app to popularize a feature worth showing off to friends is the app that people will flock to. They are the trend-setters and everyone follows them, even when there are better apps out there that do the same thing.

Herds of buffalo don't always travel in the best path. Sometimes they lead each other off of a cliff. Humans are not much different. They follow what's popular, and what's popular is not always the best choice.

App development tip #7: Figure out what's lacking out there.

When I was using the built-in iPhone browser, Safari, I had a tendency to rotate a website by accident. This usually happened when I was trying to read a news article while laying on my bed and the phone tilted enough to cause the screen to rotate. This made it hard for me to read articles, because I would then have to read lines of text sideways. That is why I added the ability to lock the screen on my browser and allow the users to choose when they want the screen to rotate. This feature was so well-received that Apple stole the idea from me (or should I say, was inspired by me), and coded the rotation-lock button in its core operating system.

The people working at Apple tend to create their own versions of an app after seeing how successful an app feature has become. For example, there have been many podcast apps out there before Apple decided to create its own podcast app. Even more recently, it is rumored that the company would release its own streaming radio app after many radio apps have already appeared in the App Store for years. So, don't expect your feature to remain exclusive for much longer. This is especially true if you do not patent the idea. But there are still perks to being the first one to introduce a feature to the world. Your app will get the news and blog coverage that will help raise awareness for your app.

15 THE BIG BREAK

It's very hard to narrow down the events of my life to exactly one big break. There was never just one big break for me. There were several points in my life that changed things forever.

If I took a step all the way back, my big break could have been when I started selling online game hacks and items for several hundreds of dollars a day. At the rate that I was earning money, I was earning more than my father was earning even though I was only 18.

Fast forward a bit, and my big break could have been when I got the job at Columbia University. Without the job, I would never have gotten the MacBook that I needed to start coding apps.

Fast forward a bit further, and it could have been when my "News Feed Elite" app became the #1 news app in 2009 (the app was later combined with my browser app and is now called "Start Up! Browser"). Using the technologies I developed from my browser app, I made an app that made it easy to view various news sites. It was successful, because it allowed you to scroll through websites by tilting your phone, save news articles to be read at a later time (even offline), block ads, share sites to Twitter/Facebook, and do other things. It basically paved the way for the other popular news apps you see today.

But if you want to look at my most successful app to date as my big break, then it would be my 5-0 Radio app. It is currently and has been the #1 police scanner app for the iPhone since it was created in 2009. To date, it has been downloaded by at least 10 million people. It has stayed in the top 10 utilities and news categories for years now, and at its peak, it was in the top 10 paid apps in various countries. People had many uses for this app from monitoring crime in their neighborhood to getting live alerts about hazards in the region to keeping in touch with family members who were in the force. People have used this app to get early tornado warnings, hurricane warnings, flood warnings, and other news before the radio and TV broadcast them. Other copycat apps have since popped up and saturated the market. However, my 5-0 Radio app is still a top seller and is among the top 100 most downloaded app in 2010 and 2011 according to Apple's end-of-the-year report.

So how did it happen? What was the big marketing secret that made it so successful?

There was no one thing that made the app super successful. It was a combination of all the tips and lifehacks that I talked about that propelled the app to the top. On one side, we have a quality product that presents itself very well. The icon was very well thought out. It was colorful, and didn't use the default icon gloss that poorly designed apps used. I spent a little bit more time on my packaging, and it made a whole lot of difference. The screenshots also showed exactly what the app did, and people got exactly what they saw and expected (and sometimes more than what they expected). On the other side, we have an app that has been marketed very well.

App development tip #8: User reviews are extremely important.

Back then, I would rely on friends and family to rate my apps to give it that extra boost in reviews and ratings. Apple has since frowned upon rigging the ratings system and has even started banning apps that do so. So instead, I created a system that now simply suggests users to rate the app. All of the popular apps do this. If the app is opened after five days and the number of uses is over fifteen, then the app automatically asks the user to review the app. The user can decline if they want to, or have the app remind them the next day.

The reason why this is important is that people tend to not review a product until they have something important to say about it. If they're satisfied with the product, then they will not make the extra effort to find your app in the App Store again just to leave a review. On the flip side, if the users are annoyed by something, then they will make the effort to make it known to the world that your app has scorned them. You would be surprised at how pissed someone can be over one dollar wasted. And these are the same people who pay five dollars for coffee.

After I implemented this system in my 5-0 Radio app, I saw my five-star ratings almost double, while my one-star ratings remained the same. The five-day waiting period and fifteen-usage threshold have effectively weeded out all those users who did not like the app. Most users delete an app after a day or two if they do not like it. They probably will also not open the app more than fifteen times. Thus, my app is only asking a subset of its users to rate the app. It is asking the users who like the app enough to keep it for more than a few days and to use it on a regular basis.

Now that 5-0 Radio is enjoying a four and a half star average rating, it basically sells itself. When people see that thousands of people are rating this app highly while only a few people are rating it poorly, they will naturally want to get the app themselves. Whenever one of my apps drops in rating, even by just half a star in the average rating, I can see the sales drop dramatically. Thus, it is always ideal to keep the rating high no matter what the cost.

If people are rating your app poorly because of a small bug, then fix that bug immediately. Reply to your customers' emails, and they will reward you with a good review of your app. Ignore them, and they will leave you with bad reviews. Give them an incentive to rate your app if they aren't rating your app. I've seen popular apps give users free levels or free virtual currency in exchange for ratings. I think this is against the terms of service from Apple, but I still see apps get away with it.

App development tip #9: Make it easy to market the app.

What I've been seeing often are apps pushing their users to "liking" their Facebook page or following their Twitter feeds. As I mentioned earlier, those are the standard procedures to growing your user base. But you should also think of clever ways to get users to help market the app for you.

For example, in my 5-0 Radio app, I implemented a chat system so that users could interact with one another while listening to the stations. But in order to use the chat system, the users had to log into their Twitter accounts. Then whenever they made a message in the chat room, it would also tweet the message on their Twitter accounts to their followers along with a #50radio hash tag. I used that hash tag as a way to track all the conversations and create a real-time chat room. I also added an "I'm listening to" button that posted the station that they were listening to along with an ad for 5-0 Radio on their Twitter feed. This type of free Twitter advertising by the users helped propel 5-0 Radio to the top. The other reason why I did this was because it saved me bandwidth by not having to implement an actual chat room on my website that would potentially be used by millions of users.

In my Police Scanner+ app, I tried a different approach. I had all the users chat by converging them to a Facebook fan page created for the Police Scanner+ app. This caused a lot of users to "like" my Facebook fan page, and now that fan page reaches thousands of Facebook users per week. All of these methods made it seamless for the user to advertise my apps for me. Some of them probably don't know that they're helping me advertise my app.

And there's no real adverse effect for making it easier for users to market the app for you. Nobody's going to leave your app a bad review for having a link to your app's Facebook page in the app. I've seen some games even unlock three extra levels if you visit their app's Facebook page. Any marketer would notice these marketing ploys, but the average user would not bat an eyelid.

App development tip #10: Use the keywords field the right way.

Some of you may already know the importance of SEO (search engine optimization). SEO is the process of raising the search-engine ranking of your website, so that it would appear at the beginning of the search engine results when certain keywords are entered. The theory is that users tend to visit the first few results first, thus increasing the visitor count for the websites that are ranked higher in the search engine results. There are entire companies dedicated to helping other companies with SEO. By the way, I would suggest avoiding these companies, because they are using strategies that you can look up yourself, or they could be involved in shady tactics. The other reason is that search engine traffic does not make up the majority of your visitors. Instead, having links on other websites to your website generates more traffic.

There are many SEO amateurs and scammers out there who only pretend that they know what they're doing, but in reality, have no idea how to really optimize your website. These people fall under the "fake it till you make it" category. They will even offer many guarantees that are basically scams that prey on people who don't know better. They may guarantee top ten rankings, but they will usually use keywords that nobody searches on. For example, let's say that your company was called Rego Apps. This is a very uncommon keyword. So, if you search "Rego Apps" on a search engine, then it will almost always be the #1 result in the search engine rankings. Thus, having guaranteed top ten rankings is meaningless unless the keyword is a frequently searched keyword. Plus, you can guarantee to have your website in the first page of results for keywords if you just pay Google a certain amount of money. For years now, companies have been outbidding each other to get their website on the top results for certain keywords. If you had the money, you could just do this yourself and save yourself from having to pay a middle man.

These SEO scammers will also try to impress you by saying that they'll submit your website to thousands of search engines. This would be impressive if people actually used those thousands of search engines equally. However, as of May 2011, over 98% of the people in this world use only the top 4 search engines (82.8% of the people use Google, 6.42% of the people use Yahoo, 4.89% of the people use Baidu, and 3.91% of the people use Bing®). Thus, you only need to submit your website to those four search engines to get results. In most cases, the major search engines will already index your website for you within a week's time (usually, within 48 hours).

There are many other scams and lies they'll tell you to get you to use to their services. Some will say that they have an inside man working at Google. Some will say that they know secret techniques that nobody else is doing. Some will say that they cracked the algorithm. These are all lies to get you to pay for their services. Only a handful of Google engineers know the algorithm, and the algorithm is changing all of the time anyway.

In general, your search engine rankings are determined by how many reputable websites link to your website and whether or not the keyword appears in your domain name, title of your website, description of your website, or in the content of your website. Every time a company figures out how to rig the system so that the website's ranking would be higher than it should be, search engine companies change their algorithm to combat the rigging. At worst, the search engines would even ban the website from their results. Thus, it is better to employ SEO methods that last longer rather than to go for the dirty techniques that some bad SEO companies offer. Such techniques, such as spamming your link on a ton of different websites, would likely get your website's ranking higher temporarily, but lower in the long run.

There are many websites out there that offer free SEO tips. It is not worth repeating them in this book, because the strategies can change at any moment anyway.

Once you have your website optimized, you must focus on iTunes' keyword search. This is how a lot of users are going to find your app, especially if your app is not in any of the top charts. Apple's algorithm is also tricky in that it changes often. However, after carefully studying it for three years now, I think I figured out how they determine the rankings in the search results.

There are two important factors to take your app to the top of the keyword search results. If your app contains the name of the keyword in your app's name, then it will be higher in the results. This is especially true if the keyword is at the beginning of the name, and even more true if it's the only word in your app's name. The second most important factor is how popular your app is. If your app is downloaded and used by many people, then it will get a higher ranking in the search results.

One of the tips that I tell people is to not waste keywords by using another popular app's name. Usually this gets your app rejected. But even if your app doesn't get rejected, it is very likely that your app will not appear near the top of the search results or in the search results at all (especially if the keyword is really popular). For example, if you use the keywords "5-0 Radio" in your keywords field, you will most likely not even see your app's results in the search results. Thus, you've wasted a keyword, and Apple only gives you a limited number of keywords to use. I tested this theory by putting those keywords in my "Police Scanner+" app. That app does not appear when you search for "5-0 Radio" at the time of this writing. Strangely, I've seen it appear occasionally when Police Scanner+ gets popular. So perhaps there's a popularity cut-off point.

Another trick I learned is that you can sneak extra characters in their keywords field. Apple normally only allows you 100 characters for keywords, and a lot of people mistakenly use spaces after a comma to separate their keywords. Those spaces count towards your

100 character limit. You can squeeze an extra keyword or two into your keywords search if you just separate your keywords with only a comma and no spaces.

16 FINAL FIGHT

There was a reason why I had to employ so many marketing tactics to promote my 5-0 Radio app. A few days before my app was released, someone else had released a similar app. We had both been developing a police scanner app at the same time while unaware of each other's work. His app quickly shot to the top while my app followed right behind his.

It became a heated battle for months as my app slowly trailed his by a few positions. However, as the months went on, the gap became larger. What had happened was that people saw that the rival app was higher ranked than 5-0 Radio and just went for the more popular one. That sucked for me, because his app was only higher ranked because he beat my release date by only a few days, and thus had an early lead.

As the gap grew larger, I feared that my app would get buried and it would have been a failed project. At that point, his app was probably making a grand or so per day, while mine was only making a few hundred. Making a few hundreds of dollars a day was still impressive, but I worked too hard on the app to let it be beaten by another person just because I didn't release it earlier. And the reason why I didn't release it earlier was because I had too many things going on in my life as well as because I wanted the app to be perfect. I'm a bit of a perfectionist, so there have been many nights when I'd stay up until 10 A.M. the next morning while still coding and tweaking the app. And my anti-procrastinator attitude also prevents me from sleeping and waiting until the next day to finish the app. Even as I write the final chapters of this book, it is all happening in the wee hours of the morning.

Finally, I decided to pull the greatest marketing tactic that I would ever attempt on an app. It was an untested marketing tactic and could have backfired on me if it didn't work. I stood a chance at losing everything if it failed, because I would lose my app's rankings and thus lose a big portion of my marketing by not being on the top charts anymore.

App development tip #11: The Hail Mary Pass.

What I'm about to teach you is something that I kept secret for about three years now. It is what I call the "Hail Mary Pass" for apps. In American football, the "Hail Mary Pass" refers to any long forward pass made usually with little success towards the end of a half. It is a desperation move used to try to score a final touchdown before the half is over or before the game is over.

This move is very similar. If it works, you could end up a multi-millionaire. And if it doesn't, then you may have shot yourself in the foot. This was a move that I made out of desperation, because I either had to beat the rival app or I'd stay behind forever.

What I did was create an identical app to 5-0 Radio with slightly less features. I removed the abilities to record and to set a sleep timer or alarm. I then started selling that app for a dollar while selling the older version for two dollars. The older version was called "5-0 Radio Pro". This was marketed as an upgrade to the regular 5-0 Radio app.

The reason why this move is dangerous is that you are splitting the download numbers between the two apps and thus lowering the individual rank per app. By having a lower rank in the App Store charts, you are losing good free marketing from Apple.

For the final step, I turned that regular one-dollar 5-0 Radio app into a free app temporarily. This was ground-breaking at the time, because no other police scanner apps were available for free. This meant that if you wanted a free police scanner app, you'd have to get my 5-0 Radio app. This became a huge hit among everyone. I tried to spread the word about the free app to as many people as possible, and those people in turn helped spread the word to other people.

The app became viral, and soon I was getting over 80,000 new users per day in just North America alone. The app quickly became the #1 app in Australia and was in the top 10 charts around the world. The way I reached #1 in Australia was that I put the words "Australian Police Scanner" after my app name. This resonated with the Australian users and they felt that they were getting an app especially designed for their country. This might serve as an anecdotal story for you to localize your app to the different regions of the world. If your app is good enough, it is worth your time to have the app translated so that you open up your business to non-English speaking customers as well.

To cash in on the popularity of the app, I also changed the 5-0 Radio Pro app to include music stations as well as railroad and airport stations. I decreased the price to one dollar and advertised the sale on the free version of 5-0 Radio. To cash in further on it, the link to the 5-0 Radio Pro app on my free version is actually an affiliate link to the App Store. Thus, I was also enjoying an extra 5% commission for every sale that I got after the customer clicked on the "Upgrade" button. This commission also included sales to other apps and songs on iTunes, as long as the user bought those things within a few minutes after using my affiliate link. So for the past few years, I've been helping Apple sell millions of dollars worth of apps and songs. An Apple employee even personally called me to congratulate me for being one of their top affiliates. At first, it didn't start off as congratulations. Instead, they called to see why I was able to sell so many apps and songs. They thought that I was cheating or spamming. When I explained to them what I was doing, they changed their tone, and now I'm one of their top salesmen. Just from the 5% commission alone, I was making way more money than what I was making at Columbia University.

The boost in recognition and sales was enough to propel my 5-0

Radio Pro app to beat popular apps such as Angry Birds and others. The marketing tactic had worked way better than expected, and I had blown way past my rival apps. Those rival apps have never recovered for the past three years, and 5-0 Radio Pro has been the #1 police scanner app for all of those years. Because of this "Hail Mary Pass", my app was making millions while my rival apps were only making hundreds of thousands.

Soon, all the rival apps tried to copy my style. They tried mimicking my icon. They tried imitating my interface and my extra features. They even tried to create their own free app to boost their sales. The problem was that they were all just imitations, and the lack of innovation did not get the users to want to switch apps. 5-0 Radio quickly became a brand name. Now when people think of police scanner apps on the iPhone, they think of 5-0 Radio.

A few years later, I decided to create a police scanner app to rival my own app. I figured that I could be both the #1 and #2 police scanner apps at the same time. There was really nothing stopping me from doing so as long as my new app looked nothing like my old one. Thus, I set out to create my Police Scanner+ app. The new app looked much sleeker and more futuristic than the 5-0 Radio app. If you compared screenshots between Police Scanner+ and 5-0 Radio, you wouldn't be able to tell that they were created by the same developer. Even my rival apps looked more similar to my 5-0 Radio app than my Police Scanner+ app did. My goal was to prove to my rivals that one could create an app that doesn't mimic 5-0 Radio's look and still become successful. I also wanted to prove to myself that I wasn't just a one-hit wonder.

The Police Scanner+ app became a success, and it could even be deemed as too successful. It started stealing users away from 5-0 Radio as well as the rival apps. But that was okay, because the two apps combined made up the majority of police scanner app users and increased my overall profits. Police Scanner+ is now among the top three police scanner apps and earns a healthy amount of money per day. And 5-0 Radio still tops the charts and still makes thousands of dollars per day.

17 THE MINDSET

A lot of you who are reading this book are probably not going to be app developers, and many of the app development strategies would not apply to your line of business. But throughout the years of interacting with other successful people, I noticed that there was still a common mindset among us. Sometimes just developing that mindset for yourself can make the difference between being successful or not. So, I leave you with some of my final thoughts on what it takes to be successful and what being successful should mean.

Lifehack #22: Be more than what society expects of you.

If you ever watch TV or movies, you'll notice a generalization that the picture perfect family is a middle-class family where the dad spends most of his time at a nine-to-five office job and his children grow up following in his footsteps and taking a similar office job.

This is what society expects of you. They want you to go to high school to prepare for college. And they want you to go to college, so that you can train for your nine-to-five job. They don't teach you how to make millions of dollars. They don't teach you how to form a limited liability company. They don't teach you much about being successful in general. And there's a reason for this. They don't expect you to amount to much, because there's a 99% chance that you will not be a part of the top 1% of income earners.

But if you look at my situation and my age, you'll see that anyone can break out of the mold and go beyond society's expectations. It took only one year for me to jump from having the median U.S. household income (around $50,000) to being above the top 0.1% income (above $1 million).

So, why did that happen? What was different about me compared to the rest of the people? It was simple. All my life, I was training and studying to have the skills to create great things. But the problem was that I wasn't working for myself. I was working for another company. I was helping another CEO/founder build his dream so that he would get rich. And I only did it, because that was what was expected of me.

Lifehack #23: Don't be a follower. Be a leader.

You should always be yourself and have faith in yourself. Don't try to mimic what other successful people are doing. Create your own thing. When other people start copying what you do, then you'll know that you're the successful one. You're the leader, and they're the followers.

According to *Millionaire Next Door* by Thomas J. Stanley, Ph.D and William D. Danko, Ph.D, self-employed people make up less than 20 percent of the workers in the U.S., but they make up two-thirds of the millionaires. This is why working for yourself and being your own boss is one of the keys to success.

As an employee, you are limited by the salary that is given to you. If the product you worked on makes millions of dollars, you're not going to be enjoying a big piece of those millions of dollars. You are stuck with a much smaller salary and occasionally a little bit of stocks in the company. You just helped make someone else millions of dollars. Thus, your income will always be capped off by how much someone is willing to pay you.

When I was working for myself in college with my first business venture, I realized that I could make so much more money by being self-employed rather than being employed by others. There was no limit to how much money I could make. I could keep working on more and more projects, and then I'd increase my income more and more each time. I was only limited by time.

Lifehack #24: Hack away the unnecessary things in your life.

Making more money each day is not as important as having more free time each day. If you have the benefit of youth, then use it. The younger you are, the more likely you have free time. Once you start a family and a career, you have less and less free time to self-educate and explore your talents. Being young also means that you have fresh ideas and are full of energy. So, let time work on your side and not against you.

Time management is probably one of the most important things you'll learn in business or even in life in general. The reason is that time is one of those things that you cannot get back. You can lose all your possessions and your money, but you can always get it all back through work. But if you lose time, there's no way to get back the time you just lost.

When wealthy and successful people hang out with me, they are not envious of my income. Instead, they are envious of my efficient time management. Anyone can make a million dollars if you gave them all the time in the world. But making a million dollars in less than a year without working at all? That takes a lot of time management skills. And one of those skills is being able to remove all the unnecessary things in your life that are taking up your time. Do you watch a lot of TV? Watch less. Do you play a lot of video games? Play less. Do you sleep for more than eight hours? Sleep less.

Tether-free Principle

Most of my free time was made possible because of my 'tether-free principle'. When I was working full-time at Columbia University, taking care of my mother, and coding apps in my spare time, I came up with a plan to eliminate as many tethers as possible in my life.

A tether is something that forces you to do a certain task either at random periods in time or at a fixed time period. A tether can be something as simple as paying your bills by mailing a check, or something as complex as holding a 9-5 job. Each of those tasks are holding you back from the free time that you could spend building your dream.

The key to true happiness is not about making the most money. It's more about having the most uninterrupted time in your life to do the things you want to do.

There are some tethers that are almost impossible to cut away. For example, you should still shower every day and go to the bathroom every day. But take advantage of that downtime and make them work for you. When I take a shower, I try to think of new app ideas, or try to figure out how to solve a bug in one of my programs. A lot of my ideas came from when I was showering. It was a relaxing part of my day, and it allowed my mind to wander and be a bit more creative. And when I was sitting on the toilet, I would spend the few minutes testing my apps out or trying other apps to see what my competitors were doing.

Another major unavoidable tether in your life may be your phone. But the impact of this tether can be reduced. For example, I don't give my phone number to just anyone. In fact, if it can be avoided, I wouldn't give my number away at all. If someone wants to contact me, I give them my email address. Your phone acts as a tether to your life. You could be working on the most important business discovery in your life, but then a friend calls you up and you two end up spending an hour chatting about nothing important. Or worse, you end up having one of those people who love texting you long paragraphs and each time you reply with one word or one sentence, they reply back with another essay.

Side note: If you're one of those people, please note that there's a reason why text messages are only 160 characters long. Please have the decency to call or put your story about your girlfriend problems in email form, so that my phone doesn't vibrate and beep every 10 seconds for the next half hour. Thank you.

And finally, when you have a successful business going, try to automate the process as much as possible. If customers are asking you the same questions over and over again, create a FAQ (frequently asked question) on your company website. After I did that for my apps, I reduced the number of customer service questions from dozens a day to maybe one or two a day. Now, all of my businesses are truly passive income.

The last major tether in my life was my full-time job. By doing office work for 40 hours a week, I was not getting the free time I wanted to expand my businesses. Thus, I had to quit my Columbia job after working there for more than two years.

Family and a social life can be tethers as well. But these would fall under necessary tethers. Family should always come first before business. You can always replace money, but you cannot replace your family. And your social life should be what keeps you happy when you're not working. Think of it as a stress reliever to your work-mode life. But keep in mind that having a girlfriend or boyfriend can be very time-consuming. When I started coding apps, I broke up with my girlfriend at the time because I wasn't giving her the time that she deserved. So when you get serious in your business, there may come a time when you have to choose between your work and your significant other. What's better is if your girlfriend/boyfriend understands that you need time to work on your projects, and doesn't interfere with your work.

One way to measure how successful you really are is by seeing how much time you need to spend working. I know many doctors and lawyers who are wealthy, but they are married to their work. As soon as they stop working, their income drops as well. They are tethered to their work even though they are considered by society as "wealthy". But what kind of life would that be if you cannot spend time enjoying your wealth?

If I disappeared from the face of the Earth for a year, my income would still stay consistent. Even all of my bills are automatically being drafted from my checking accounts. And all of my income automatically gets deposited into my checking accounts.

When you reach that level of free time, the possibilities for creating new business ventures and/or enjoying your life are endless.

Lifehack #25: Don't put all of your eggs in one basket.

This falls in line with the concept that you should diversify your investments. Except this time, I want to talk about diversifying your income. At the time of this writing, I have over a dozen different sources of income. This is because you will never know when you will suddenly lose a source of income, especially if someone has control over your income. And this was a lesson I learned the hard way.

Before my 5-0 Radio app became successful, I had set up a Google AdSense account for my company. I put the mobile ads on my website and everything was fine. However, after my 5-0 Radio blew up and went viral, people started hammering my company website. This uptick in new visitors caused my AdSense account to go from earning a few hundreds of dollars a day to suddenly a few thousands of dollars a day. This must have raised a red flag in the AdSense system, because after sustaining thousands of dollars a day in revenue for a while, Google banned my company's AdSense account for having invalid clicks. I appealed the decision and explained that my app had gone viral. I only got a cookie-cutter response back from them along with their denial of my appeal.

That was a devastating blow, because it took out about a fourth of my income. To add insult to injury, Google even kept the past two and a half months of revenue and never paid me for all the earnings I earned prior to my 5-0 Radio app's popularity explosion. I think they owed me around $100,000 when all was said and done. It was the most money I had ever lost in a day.

Ever since then, I decided to stay away from AdSense for my apps and their no-tolerance policies. I now use about half a dozen different advertisement companies to advertise on my websites. The amount they pay me isn't as high as what Google paid me, but at least they don't randomly ban my account because of sudden spikes in user clicks. In fact, all the advertisement companies that I now work with all know me personally. They all beg for me to give them more ad inventory, because of my millions of ad impressions per day.

There was even a day when the Vice President of Quattro Wireless (now called iAd) called me personally to congratulate me for my success and for the business I gave them. He even asked if he could meet me in person at an Apple developer event called WWDC. This happened after I earned $70,000 worth of ad revenue in a week through Quattro Wireless. Since the advertisement revenue was split at around 50-50 at the time, it meant that I single-handedly helped their company raise $35,000 in a week.

That $35,000 could have gone to Google. But Google's ban left a sour taste in my mouth, and I decided to never help Google again. That is the sole reason why I never developed a single Android® app, even though I could be earning more revenue if I had done so. The only way I'd forgive them is if they helped me earn back the $100,000 that they denied me. Having the uncertainty of getting banned again made my life stressful, and it wasn't worth the extra money. I remember that every email I got from Google gave me chills, because I didn't know what other bad news they had to give me.

Ever since then, I learned to treat each successful day like it was my last.

They say that you should treat every day like it is your last, so that you would appreciate your day more. Once you keep having successful days, you may start to lose motivation to work further. It is very easy to rest on your laurels when you have achieved greatness (especially when you get it fast and at a young age).

So instead, I pretended that each day was the last day I'd be earning a lot of money. Because of this mentality, I get to wake up each day feeling as though I won the lottery. That way, I stay humble, and only spend what I've already earned. And even then, I'd be wary of spending, because I'd rather save and invest the lottery winnings.

18 DEALING WITH SUCCESS

I haven't actively sought fame since I was 19. Ever since that incident with GunBound, I figured that it was better to be successful anonymously. Even when news outlets like CNN, ABC, NBC, and FOX News wanted to do interviews with me over my apps, I dodged them. It was the apps that people were buying, and not me. I didn't think it was worth it to sell out my privacy for more money.

If seeking and gaining attention is what makes you happy, then you are getting yourself onto a slippery slope. Fame is dangerous in that it never lasts. You may be on the front cover of magazines one day, and then become a has-been the next day. Fame is also a double-edged sword. While fame can help you sell your products, it can also attract jealous people who want nothing but to take you down for being successful.

You should also be careful about using exotic cars as your motivation for success. Being motivated by expensive material goods is unfulfilling. Once you've own the exotic car that you want, you will get used to the feeling within a year or so. It will not stay as a constant source of happiness.

Lifehack #26: Be true to yourself and own it. Don't be a poser.

If you really must own an exotic car to be happy, then you might be glad to hear that it doesn't take much to own an exotic car these days. You can even buy a Lamborghini Gallardo for less than $90,000 if it is old (more than 7 years old) and has high-mileage (above 20,000). And if you think that $90,000 is expensive, then you have to remember that the true cost of owning a car is how much you're paying for maintenance, gas and depreciation. Thus, if you buy a $90,000 Lamborghini and then turn around and sell it for $90,000 a few months later without spending any money on the car, then you've pretty much owned a Lamborghini for free. And if you have connections with a car dealer, then you can even go to car auctions and buy used cars at wholesale prices. Then without ever registering the car under your name, you can drive those used cars without ever paying taxes. And even if you do plan on registering the car under your name, you can set up a limited-liability company in Montana (a state with no sales tax), and buy and sell cars under that company without ever having to pay taxes on it.

You could do all of that as well, but then you'd just be seen as poser. And if you're okay with that label, then you might want to start evaluating your goals in life. Are you doing this for your ego? Are you doing this for the fame and attention? All of these reasons are signs of low self-esteem, and a lot of people will see through it. There may be gullible teenagers who buy into it, but everyone else will call you out on it and see you as disingenuous.

I know people who buy used Lamborghini's without even owning their own house first. Usually it's the younger, egotistical kids with wealthy parents who do these things. But can you blame them? They live under the shadow of their wealthy parents. That makes them desperate to become successful or at least appear successful, because that's what's expected of them. They also have wealthy peers who compete with them in pissing contests, so they're always trying to show off to keep up with appearances. Since their parents lavish them with gifts, they are used to getting what they want when they want. It's this "spoiled brat" attitude that causes them to keep buying high-end cars and other luxurious things with no remorse. They feel as though it is their privilege, and nobody is going to say no to them.

They'll also lie and cover up facts to create the illusion that they are more successful than they actually are. They care more about their status than most people do. They make a little money in their business at a young age and then spend it all on cars while living under their parents' roof. Financially, a wealthy person would choose an appreciating asset like real estate over a depreciating asset like a high-end exotic car. So these people aren't making wise financial decisions. They're simply buying these cars as status symbols.

There's this one teenager I know from the exotic car forums who does this. He comes from a family of wealth and goes through Lamborghini's like they were clothes. He had a connection with a car dealer (presumably through his family connections) and was able drive Lamborghini's with very little financial loss. He barely kept any car for more than a few months, because he would have to sell the car before it depreciates. I've lost count of how many Lamborghini's he has owned, but it is around a dozen or so. What amazes me the most is that he's still a teenager at the time of this writing.

That's the true story behind his cars, but he'll never tell you that. He leaves out all of these details, because he wants you to believe that he's successful at his business. But the truth is that his business is not even doing that well for him to afford multiple Lamborghini's. And although he'll take all the credit for his business, he'll leave out the fact that his wealthy parents were the ones who invested it and gave him help. This gave the illusion that he earned all of the success by himself. A lot of people fell for it at first, but as more people looked further into it, they realized that this guy was actually just a poser. He pretty much lost all credibility when he constantly kept bragging about buying this and that without actually going through with it.

The lesson here is that you should not be this poser when you come across a little bit of wealth. You should either be honest about your financial situation or don't tell people at all. Just don't lead them into believing that you are more successful than you actually are. It will backfire on you when people find out the truth. And the truth will come out eventually. It came out for this kid after a few months, and now he's pretty much the laughing stock of the car forums (whether he realizes it or not).

Lifehack #27: Be confident, not conceited.

Having confidence is important in all aspects of life. Whether you're in a business meeting setting up a new partnership or in a bar trying to attract a girl, confidence is the trait that people look for. However, some people, especially those with a little bit of success, end up coming off as being conceited rather than confident. And being conceited is not a very good look on a person. So how can you tell if a person is being confident or being conceited?

Confident people are people who can laugh at themselves. If they can take a joke about their weaknesses, then they're showing signs of confidence. On the other hand, a conceited person doesn't take criticism very well. He will try to hide his insecurities and even get defensive and angry if you point out his flaws. He may try to downplay the effects that the criticisms have on him, but he is secretly dwelling on it for days and even months. You wouldn't know it until months later when he gets defensive about the criticisms and starts ranting about haters and what not.

Confident people are people who adhere to moral and ethical principles. They don't resort to doing immoral things to get what they want. They don't choose profits over friends and fans. They have their priorities straight. Thus, if a person lacks integrity, then he is not a confident person. A conceited person is one who relies on drugs, women, and/or fancy cars to feel important. That's because conceited people are the ones who are insecure and self-conscious about how others view them. So if the person is constantly showing off his girlfriends, cars, and expensive purchases, then he is conceited and not confident.

Conceited people also like being better than the people around them. They set their goals based on what other people are doing. If his friend gets an expensive car, then he feels the need to get an even more expensive car. They like to compare themselves to others because they feel insecure about themselves. And they are always trying to show that they are better than other people in order to cover their insecurities. Confident people don't need to compare themselves to others. They only aim for standards that they set for themselves.

Confident people also take pleasure from praising other people. Conceited people only talk about how good they are. They are not secure enough to admit that some people are better than them at something. Thus, they rather talk about their strengths while pointing out the weaknesses in others.

Conceited people are also close-minded. If you try to correct them, they will ignore you. If you try to advise them on something, they will ignore you. If you try to teach them something, they will ignore you. Conceited people think that they're great the way they are and don't need to improve themselves further. They always think that they're right, and they'll find excuses when they realize that they're wrong. They will shift the blame onto others for being wrong. And they will make up a B.S. answer when they don't know the answer to something. Confident people, on the other hand, know that they have room for improvement. They enjoy learning from others, and know when to admit that they don't know something.

The even more conceited ones are those who are so insecure that they try to cover up their conceitedness. They are afraid that people will call them out on their arrogance, so they resort to sneaky tactics to hide their conceitedness.

These sneaky conceited people will use dishonesty to deceive others. They are obsessed with people's views on them, so they will make up lies about themselves. Or if they fear getting caught, they will purposefully be ambiguous about something and let you make assumptions about them. And when you ask whether your assumptions are correct, conceited people will not give you an answer, because they want you to believe in your false assumptions that favor them. They don't want to admit to making purposefully deceiving statements. For example, they'll talk about how they made money on their early projects, and then show off their expensive things. They want you to assume that they could afford those expensive things because of the money they earned from their early projects. But in reality, their early projects didn't actually make that much money to afford them their expensive purchases. So when you ask them about how much money their early projects made, they will either dodge your question or lie. But if you ask people in the same line of business or the people who worked with them on those projects, you'll find out the truth and realized that these conceited people were being deceitful by leaving out the facts.

The sneakier conceited people will also label themselves inappropriately. They will call themselves CEOs of a company, even though that company only consists of one employee. They know that people associate CEOs with success and wealth, so they are actually trying to label themselves as successful and wealthy. But the truth is that anyone can start their own company for a few hundred dollars and call themselves the CEO of it. Those who know that their company isn't all that great will be able to see through this poorly-veiled attempt at deceit.

The sneakier conceited people also love to humblebrag. By this I mean that they subtly brag about how wonderful their lives are while making seemingly humble, self-depreciating statements. For example, they'll say something along the lines of, "The champagne on this first-class flight to Paris tastes horrible." While they want you to believe that the horrible champagne they're having is the focus of that statement, what they really want you to know is that they are on a first-class flight to Paris.

Some other tricks that the sneakier conceited people use are taking pictures that show off their wealth. They will then caption those pictures without talking about the thing that they are really trying to show off. It is their way of humblebragging through images. For example, a person can take a picture of his shoes while sitting in the front row seats at a NBA game, and only talk about how his shoes look in the photo captions. What the person is trying to do is show off his front row seats to an NBA game without appearing as though he is showing off.

The sneakier conceited people also use false modesty. When you praise them, they will purposefully refuse praise just so that they can hear it again. For example, if you tell a conceited girl that you think she's really pretty, she'll say something along the lines of, "Huh? You think I'm pretty? I'm not that pretty." This can actually be false modesty. She may be fishing for more compliments. A confident person would instead turn the conversation around and start praising the other person.

There is no need to be conceited to become or feel successful. Only the weak must resort to bragging to feel significant, while the confident ones don't. It's much like how only the small dogs feel the need to bark to look fierce, while the big dogs don't.

Lifehack #28: Try to avoid depending on validation from others.

"I'm not in this world to live up to your expectations and you're not in this world to live up to mine." – Bruce Lee

One of the keys to being rich is staying humble. I know a lot of young people who obtain wealth really quickly and then blow it all while thinking that money comes by easily. Once their income stops or slows, they end up with a bunch of bills and expensive toys that they can no longer afford. Their shopping sprees fueled their ego, and their ego kept them happy. But as their ego grew, it took more spending to keep them happy and keep them feeling as though they were progressing. However, a lot of times that ego also keeps them from doing productive work.

Ever notice that a lot of famous music artists only make one or two great songs and then are never heard from again? They got so used to partying and not working that they don't feel motivated to work hard any longer. And you can't blame them either. The record labels usually push them to go to venues after venues until they're burnt out and need an outlet for their stress. That outlet changes from person to person. Sometimes it's drugs. Sometimes it's women. Sometimes it's throwing expensive parties.

In any case, spending money is what eases their pain. And if someone is insecure as well, then he's spending the money in hopes of validation. This may be someone who people look negatively upon, so his self-esteem is so low that he resorts to showing off his wealth in exchange for validation. Often this is someone who posts pictures of his cash, cars, boats, receipts for drinks at a club, and other spending sprees on Facebook and other social networks. (Note: If it's a girl, usually she seeks validation via posted pictures of her body in cutesy poses with duck faces, or in slutty, look-down-my-shirt poses with cleavage showing. As an alternative, she will posts picture of her food, pets, baby, niece and/or nephew.)

Almost everyone will once in a while post one of these "validation" posts on Facebook. But the problem is with someone who depends on them.

The problem usually starts when the person's normal status posts get very little "likes" while his pictures of wealth gets a lot of "likes". This influences him into thinking that he can only get approval from his friends and strangers if he spends more money and talks about it.

But those "likes" are only temporary, and soon he needs to post more pictures of wealth for more "likes". Then when he realizes that different pictures of the same thing doesn't get that many new "likes", he decides to spend more money and show pictures of that. That's when the dependency starts. He starts posting only pictures that show off his wealth, and brags about what cool "baller" things he is doing. And every once in a while, he needs a fix and posts more. This is someone who gets addicted to "likes", and is emotionally attached to other people's validation of him.

This isn't the way to live your life. The only person whose validation you need is your own. You don't have to prove anything to anyone. And don't be the fool who spends a lot of his money just to prove others wrong.

Lifehack #29: Share your success.

So what purpose does earning money serve? For me, the money goes to benefiting my family and making sure that they're taken care of. It's a worthy cause that doesn't make me feel guilty in the end. Since my brother doesn't earn as much as I do, I give him and his wife a few grand a month so that his family could live a better life. I figured that a few grand a month would mean more to him than it would to me.

I admit that there are days when I feel guilty about splurging on two flashy Lamborghini's, with one worth more than double the previous. And there are days when I feel guilty about owning more than one house. But in the end, it's about what you do with these things that matter the most. Are you buying these things to show off your wealth? Or is there a more moral reason?

The reason why I bought the Lamborghini was that I eventually became overwhelmed with juggling a full time job, creating apps on the side, taking care of my mother, and maintaining a social life. Having a brand new Verde Ithaca Lamborghini Gallardo LP560-4 was my way of dealing with the stress. I know, I know, I could have just gotten a stress ball for much less. But it was my dream car, and so far, it had done a great job at putting a smile on my face each time I drove it.

The car had also put a smile on everyone else's face, and helped raised money for many charity events, so it still went along with my ideals of making this world a better place. Before the car, I never really spent any of the money I earned on myself (I was living with my mother and the Lamborghini was the very first car I bought). My mother, who's very fiscally conservative, abhorred the idea that I was getting an overly expensive and flashy car. But my brother later told me that when I was taking delivery of my new Lamborghini, my mother had a proud look on her face and even became a little teary-eyed.

And now I have a new one-of-one azure blue Lamborghini Aventador® LP700-4. I saw this car as an upgrade to my LP560, and I wanted to get rid of the flashy lime green color (the azure blue color is a much more classy color). When I took delivery of the car in

Orlando, FL, I had brought my mother with me again. It was also her first time in Florida for over twenty years, and it was her first time visiting my new big house in Florida. She never liked the idea that I was spending so much money on these luxury things, but she did not know that I was also spending the money for her.

You see, my mother suffers from catatonic schizophrenia, a very serious mental illness that she had since she was in her 20's. Stressful events in her life trigger her psychotic episodes, where she would have auditory hallucinations, have trouble expressing herself and become extremely paranoid. These psychotic episodes usually last for maybe a few days, or two weeks at most. Our family mostly dealt with it without medication for decades. Her psychiatrist said that it's possible that she developed it because she grew up in the slums, and her brother and father used to abuse her.

When my father's life was unexpectedly taken away from him, my mother's stress level shot up through the roof. She had become stuck in a psychotic episode ever since. Now instead of having just a week of catatonia, my mother is lucky to have a week where she doesn't have catatonia.

Probably one of the saddest experiences I've ever had was when my mother tried to communicate with me, but the words wouldn't come out of her mouth. Her lips would quiver and her hands would physically shake as she fought to express herself. But ultimately, she couldn't, so she started crying. I couldn't hold back my tears after witnessing this, and I started crying as well. It became common for me to spend close to six to ten hours with my mother, waiting for her to say what she had to say, or waiting for her to eat her food.

Finally, she said something.

"Maybe... maybe... I should stop being a burden to you," she spoke softly to me in Chinese. I knew what that meant. She loved me enough that she wanted to end her life to save me from being depressed and stressed after seeing her like this and after taking care of her. Something had to be done to save her.

I had tried to get her on anti-psychotic medication, but she would stop taking them after a while and would even secretly throw them away. I knew then that the only thing I could do was to institutionalize her and force her to take her medication, or to try to remove all the stresses from her life. I chose the latter.

I quickly tried to hack away all the stressful events in her life. There was even a fire in the house that my mother rented out a little more than two years after my father passed away. The fire triggered a house inspection from the city. The inspection brought a court order to fix the housing violations. It was stressful for her to deal with, so I took care of all the paperwork for the violations and for the home insurance.

The violations were unfounded. The tenants later told us that the inspector did not even look at the house. He just wrote up random violations that he assumed were there. For example, one of the violations claimed that there was a three-piece bathroom in the basement of the house (i.e. a bathroom with a sink, a toilet, and a bathtub). There was no such bathroom in the basement. There was only a toilet in the basement. The case was eventually dismissed.

But I still had to wake up at six in the morning and take my catatonic mother with me to court to fight the case. I couldn't just go alone, because I did not have the power of attorney at the time. I didn't have it because it was in short notice, and because it was close to impossible to get my mother to sign anything when she was paranoid and catatonic. At the court, my mother kept trying to drag me out because she was paranoid and scared of the unfamiliar place. Luckily, someone else was there who spoke Chinese and helped calm my mother down. But that was only temporary. After the fire, she stayed in a psychotic episode for over half a year. It was the longest she went without ever returning back to normal. I had feared that I lost my normal mother forever.

There were many more similarly stressful and unfortunate events that happened to our family. Each time, I had to stay strong to keep my mother sane and alive. My brother was (and still is) stuck in London with his wife, so I was the only one left to take care of my mother.

Finally, after months of dealing with her long-term psychotic episode, she snapped out of it. I had removed all stressors in her life. I even went out to buy her groceries with her on a weekly basis. On the days when she was too paranoid to leave the house, I would go out and buy the groceries for her. She only wanted Chinese groceries, so I had to venture out further to get them for her. During the days when she wasn't psychotic, I went down to Florida to buy a large luxurious house. By living in Florida, I reduced my income taxes. In

New York City, state and city income tax added up to around 13%. In Florida, there was no state income tax at all. The other reason why I bought a big house was because I wanted to get my mother to live in a more comfortable and relaxing home. We had been living in our small New York suburban home for decades, and it was time for me to spend some money to save my mother.

I finally convinced my mother to come down to Florida recently, and it was one of the greatest moves I had ever made for my mother's mental health. Her eyes lit up when she saw how beautiful my house was, and she was extremely relaxed and unstressed. She liked the people in Florida better than the people in New York. In New York, the people were ruder and more jaded. Here, in my small town in Orlando, FL, the people were much more polite, and she no longer felt paranoid around strangers.

I took her to Disney World and many other places. It's been over two decades since she had been to Disney World. She vaguely remembered pieces of Disney World from her past, and it helped bring out the playful and cheerful child in her. I even went on Splash Mountain with her, and she had a blast.

Because of the many amenities in my Florida house, my mother was able to stay more active than when she was in her small house in New York. She used my pool almost daily, even though she didn't know how to swim. I tried teaching her, and she was willing to learn. She took up interest in billiards and ping pong. I tried teaching her those as well, and she was willing to learn.

Because my mother was feeling lonely after the loss of my father, I adopted a small poodle from the Florida Poodle Rescue organization to help keep her company. My poodle, who I named Lambo, was originally a stray dog from Miami full of fleas. He also had an eye ulcer on his right eye, which would permanently leave him partially blinded. I had nursed him back to health, and now he's as happy as he could be.

My mother, too, was really happy. I finally got my normal, happy mother back, and I couldn't be more relieved and glad. I took her to Sea World on her birthday in September 2012. She had never been there before. The day turned out really perfect, because she loved animals as much as I did. During the middle of the day, she kissed me on the cheek. Keep in mind that my mother is very conservative and not intimate at all. She even shies away when I try to hug her. So I cannot emphasize how extremely unexpected that expression of affection was to me. After she planted the kiss, she said to me in Chinese, "Thank you for taking care of me and taking me to Sea World on my birthday. I understand that you could be doing so many other things like working on your programs or your book, but you chose to stick around. If it wasn't for you, I'd be sitting at home in New York alone on my birthday. Thank you."

The pleasure is all mine, mom. Thank you for raising me and giving me a chance at a fulfilling life. And thank you, brother, for lending your ear when I needed someone to talk to. And thank you, dad, for giving me the tools in life to be able to take care of others. And thank you, friends and readers, for listening to my family's story and for supporting my family and me.

Thank you all.

"Real living is living for others. Be happy, but never satisfied."

– Bruce Lee

In Memory of My Father

SEPT. 7, 1946 – OCT. 5, 2007

FREQUENTLY ASKED APP QUESTIONS

How do I go about learning how to code apps?

If you have the money, then take an online course or hire a tutor. Otherwise, you'll have to find free tutorial material online to learn from or take a class if your public school offers it. Learning how to code apps on your own can be difficult, especially if you have not had prior coding experience. But if you have some experience in coding, then you can probably learn how to code apps by getting a book on it (either buying it or borrowing it from the library). The only problem with books is that if you have a question, the book might not have a clear answer for you.

Once you know the basics, the best way to learn is to keep practicing. Try coding something simple at first. Something as simple as getting the screen to display the text, "Hello, World!" can be your first program. That should build up your confidence to learn more. If you try to code something difficult in the beginning, it'll be too daunting. As you code more and more programs, you'll naturally want to see what else your code can do. And that's when you'll want to keep doing more and more advanced coding.

And if you don't have that urge to do more complex coding even though you know it'll be difficult, then coding might not be for you. When I see a difficult coding task, I see it as a challenge. It's a really rewarding feeling when you actually get something to do exactly as you want it to do. In a way, it's like playing God. You created it, and now you get to see your creation thrive. Once you know how to code, there are limitless possibilities on what you can do with it.

So if you've been meaning to learn how to code, give it a try. Don't wait until next year. Don't wait until next month. Just go on your favorite search engine and start looking for coding tutorials. There are plenty of free ones out there. The sooner you start learning, the sooner you can start selling your apps or programs for profit.

Here's how I motivate myself to not procrastinate on my apps: Since some of my apps make thousands of dollars a day, I ask myself, what if I delayed one of those apps by a day? I'd lose a day of sales. And I'd never be able to turn back the clock to get those thousands of dollars worth of sales. I basically lost a few thousands of dollars, because I delayed the release of my app by a day. If I delayed it by a week, I'd lose tens of thousands of dollars. If I delayed it by a month, I'd lose hundreds of thousands of dollars. By putting that into perspective, I get motivated to stay up all night to finish that app one day sooner or one week sooner or one month sooner.

My mindset is so honed to success that I almost always feel guilty when I'm having fun and not working. I think to myself, "I could be working right now and making more money instead of watching this movie or playing this video game." The only way I can stop myself from feeling guilty is by doing those fun things with someone I care about. Then it becomes a selfless act. For example, if I took my mother to Disney World for a week, then I could enjoy it and not feel guilty about not working as well. I still have my priorities straight, because I'm putting family before work, instead of fun before work.

I have an idea for an app. Will you code it for me or recommend someone who can?

The truth is that an idea for an app isn't worth much. Anyone can come up with an idea for an app. The real difficult part is the coding, graphics, and marketing. So, unless you bring something to the table other than just an idea, then no app developer will want to work with you. You can bring money to the table, but keep in mind that apps can be expensive. There is a shortage of competent app developers for hire, because most of the large firms have picked them up or they're working on their own projects. Also keep in mind that your app may not make back the money that you paid for it. If your app fails to take off, you'll probably end up making only a few dollars on the app. And since most apps cost thousands of dollars to make, then you're already starting from a deep hole.

The projects I like to work on are with other competent people. I can do graphics, coding, and marketing all at the same time, so I work best as a consultant or someone who can fill in the gap for a missing team member. I have a proven track record on successful apps, so I don't really come cheap either.

I don't have recommendations on who to hire, since I've been doing all of my work myself, and never had to hire anyone. I would highly recommend looking at someone's portfolio before you hire them. Also, you should make sure that the price is negotiated before you start the project. There are greedy coders out there who will low-ball the price of the project to get you to hire them. But then, they'll say that the project is taking longer than they expected and expect you to pay more. And since you already paid for most of the project, then you'll have no choice but to pay them more to finish the project. Don't fall for this trap.

How do I know if my app will be successful or not?

You will not know until you actually release the app. If you have features that people are looking for and have little competition, then you probably have a successful app. Sometimes apps are only successful for a short period of time. For example, if you create an app about the U.S. Presidential election, then it will probably be popular around the time when there is an election.

Once you release the app, you will know within the first week (even the first 2 days) whether your app is a success or not. If your app fails to get into the top charts of any category, then it will not be able to self-promote itself. You will be stuck trying to promote the app yourself (perhaps through forums or social media). However, I would suggest you figure out why nobody is downloading your app in the first place before you promote your app further. The only time you should be promoting app intensely is when you know your app is actually desirable. Otherwise, you'll be wasting your time promoting an app that nobody wants when you could be spending that time coding features into the app that would make people want to get that app.

You'll also know if your app is successful or not by looking at the user reviews. If you are constantly getting 5-star reviews (maybe one or two a day) with very few negative reviews, then you have a great app that's worth promoting. But if you get more negative reviews than positive ones, then you should either scrap the idea or keep improving the app until it got to the point where people like using it.

Would you rather improve upon popular apps or go with an original idea?

Coming up with an original idea poses a greater risk, but bigger reward. There is a chance that the market doesn't want what your idea provides. And someone might steal your idea and compete against you. If you look at any of the current popular things, you'll notice that they were all stolen ideas (e.g. Facebook was not the first to do social networking, Google was not the first search engine, the iPhone was not the first smartphone, and the iPod® was not the first mp3 player).

It also worries me that if an idea hasn't been popular yet, then there might just be no demand for it. Necessity is the mother of all inventions as they say. But if you truly have an original idea that you think will be a big hit, then by all means, try it (and even patent it if you can). Even my 5-0 Radio has been emulated many times, and those competitors are making somewhat decent money by mooching off the popularity of my app. So I'd definitely say it is much safer to improve upon an existing popular app and compete. That's the basis of capitalism after all.

But if you want to make the big money, then you'll have to take the risk and release an app that nobody has made popular before. By this I mean that the idea can still be unoriginal, but it must be an idea that isn't already popular. Most of the time, people will see your app as a knock-off and not download it. It's very hard to get people to switch from what they're used to.

How do I get the initial reviews for my apps?

If you read my book, you'll already know how important it is to have a high average rating for your app. But the problem is that when first release an app, you will not have an average rating until you get at least five or so ratings. And without that average rating, people will not know how awesome your app is.

Fear not. You can get your friends and family to download the app and leave reviews for your app. But keep in mind that if they use a promo code, there's a high chance that they will not be able to leave a review. You might be better off making the app free for a day to get your friends to download the app for free at first and leave a review.

If you do not have friends and family to help you, then you can leave reviews for your own app. I would highly suggest against this, because if Apple catches you doing this, then they will ban your app or even your account. But if you're willing to take the risk, then you're going to have to create a lot of iTunes accounts to get your ratings up. To create an iTunes account for free, you just need to have an email address. Try to download a free app while logged out and you'll get a chance to create an iTunes account without entering your credit card information. Apple will then ask you to confirm your account information. You can only confirm up to three accounts per device (whether it's an iPad, iPhone, or computer). The trick is that you can go to your local electronics store that demo Apple devices. Validate your accounts through their test devices. Almost any device that can load iTunes can help you validate your account.

Keep in mind that Apple changes their procedures frequently, so these methods may no longer work in the future. But at the time of this writing, they are verified as working.

FREQUENTLY ASKED LIFE QUESTIONS

If I'm starting from scratch, what should I be doing to become wealthy?

Your focus should not be on getting wealthy. I did not start any of my ventures because I expected to get wealthy. I did what I enjoyed and it bled into my work.

In fact, I know more people who think their projects will make them millions, but end up with projects that make close to nothing. So, focus on getting a stable job first. This will ensure that you are paying rent and putting food on the table. This is something that wealthy kids can skip, because they have financial backing from their parents. They have that advantage over us, the ones with more humble beginnings. But don't let that deter you from ever trying break out of your financial class.

If you are starting from scratch, you should get yourself a good job first to pay the bills. Afterwards, use your spare time to pursue your side businesses. Find your strengths or create new ones. If people love what you do, then they will naturally want to pay for it.

For example, if you are good at making websites, then eventually, people will want to pay you to create a website for them.

Once your side businesses start making more money than your full-time job, then that's when you need to make that tough decision of whether you should focus all of your time on your side business or continue it as a part-time job only. It took me over a year before I became confident that my app business was going to generate income for a long period of time. When it comes to sales, you will never know when your business will flop, and you end up with little to no income. Thus, I didn't want to risk losing my great job at Columbia until I was sure that my iPhone apps would stay popular for longer than just a few months. And that's really something that rarely happens. I know a few developers who made hundreds of thousands of dollars the first few months that they released an app, and then they quit their full-time jobs. Later on, people stopped downloading their apps and they started making less than what they made prior to quitting their jobs. Worse off were the ones who already spent the fortune they earned on luxurious things and ended up having to sell them at a loss, because they could no longer afford to keep them.

Becoming wealthy should be a side effect of your work. If you start getting greedy, it might negatively impact your work. It is also very rare for someone to get wealthy in the first place, so that is why I always tell people to do what they love doing. That passion for your work will show in your projects. And even if you did not get wealthy from doing what you love, you will have at least enjoyed what you did. And that is more important than getting wealthy. The greatest thing you'll enjoy with successful life is not a fancy car or a nice house. Instead, you'll be enjoying the fact that you are rarely doing what I don't enjoy doing.

So find something you love doing, and make a hobby out of it. Then figure out a way to monetize it to turn it into a small business. I can't really tell you what that is, because it's hard to predict whether a business will be successful or not. If you make something that you would find useful yourself, then there is bound to be other people who would find what you made useful as well. Those will be your first customers in your path to getting wealthy.

Let's fast forward and assume that you already got your life sorted out. Here are some more tips on choosing the right path to becoming successful:

1. It is easier to become successful by working for yourself, because your income is only limited by how hard you work rather than by what your company wants to pay you.

2. It is also easier to become wealthy by selling your products to the general population rather than doing services for individuals. Those who do services for individuals are limited by how much time they have. Those who sell products to the general population are only limited by how many people are in the world with disposable income (there are a lot of those).

3. Network. The more people you know, the more help you can get in starting/expanding your business. Just be wary about surrounding yourself people who don't know what they're talking

about and don't "walk-the-walk". There are a lot of posers out there who will do nothing but waste your time and/or money.

4. Don't buy things you do not need, but invest in things worth investing in. The more money you save, the quicker you become wealthy. Save/invest money here and there, and you will accumulate more and more wealth.

The list goes on for the things you can do to get wealthy. You will find the rest of the tips by reviewing this book.

Do I need to go to college to become successful?

College is part of the methodical stage that society pushes you to go to. It is a boot camp for the office job that society wants you to take. But if you don't go to college, are you doomed to fail?

Your knowledge is limited by your own ambitions and not limited by your choice of schooling. This means that you can still self-educate yourself to fulfill your ambitions (as long as your career path doesn't require a license to operate). If you plan on becoming a doctor or a lawyer (both of which require graduate schooling and licenses), then yes, you should go to college. But what if your ambition is to become an app developer like me? I can tell you that I could have learned how to code apps without going to college. College actually never taught me anything about coding apps. Apps weren't even around until after I graduated.

Keep in mind that colleges are still a business, and they've effectively drilled the notion into our minds that knowledge and an opportunity at a good job must be bought for $100,000. It is not true, and many successful college drop-outs can attest to that. Parents who've never been to college see their friends go to college and make lots of money. So, they send their kids to college without paying for it. They're hoping that their kids could make a lot of money like their college-educated peers. However, colleges should be for intellectuals. An idiot with a degree is still an idiot. The difference is that that idiot is now drowning in debt for a piece of paper that nobody cares about.

What the parents don't realize is that their college-educated peers are making a lot of money because they are smart and/or experienced. It's not because they have degrees. I've seen many lazy people go to college just to take an easy major, party, and have fun. And now they're unemployed (or at a low-paying job) and asking why the "American Dream" is dead. It's not dead at all. It's just that you have to be smart, motivated, and really work at it.

And having a degree in a major that isn't in great demand is pretty much useless. So, going to college is not as big of a deal as it used to be. Almost anyone can get a college degree nowadays. It's much more impressive to have a full resume. Employers rather hire someone who actually applied what he learned in the real world. Is it necessary to go to college to have a full resume? Not necessarily. Is it necessary to go to college to be successful? Nope.

Think of college as training wheels. Whether you need them or not is up to you and how well you are at self-education. Also think of college as a safety net. If your ambitions fail, at least you have a college degree to fall back on to get yourself a decent job. Also college is a place where you can build connections and meet like-minded people. Just make sure to weigh that against the hefty price tag that a college degree comes with.

Isn't getting rich just based on luck?

Luck is just the starting point to great things. There comes a point early on when it stops being about luck and more about what the person did with that luck.

Let's take a look at Bill Gates' case. Some may say that he's lucky, because he was born into an upper-middle-class American family. His family had the resources to send him to private school while other families didn't. And they just so happened to send him to Lakeside School in Seattle, a school which had a Teletype connection to a computer (something rare for that era). There, he was able to learn how to program. That's where people point to when they say he got lucky. But doesn't that mean a lot of other people are lucky, too?

You see, there were many kids who went to that same school. But did they all end up becoming a billionaire? Was Bill Gates the only one who learned how to program? Was he the only one born into an upper-middle-class family? You have take into account the personal side of things as well. Give the guy some credit for actually taking the opportunity and running with it. There were many people who could have done the same, but they didn't. Just like how there are many people who could have learned how to program in Objective-C and could have made millions of dollars from apps. I wasn't the only one who was allowed to make apps. I was no luckier than the next guy. I might even argue that my life has been a series of unlucky events.

So, it's not about whether a person is lucky or not. We all get good luck and bad luck. It's about what you do when it's your lucky day and opportunity comes knocking. Do you take risks? Do you make the right choices? The difference between me and the next guy is that I look at every opportunity and I run with it. I don't quit when the going gets tough. I stare at mountains and I say, "Yea, I can climb that." Usually, my body quits on me before my mind does. When I work out, I don't quit because I can't stand the pain. I quit when my body physically cannot work out anymore. When I code, I don't quit because the programming is too difficult. I quit because I fell asleep on the keyboard. Some call it OCD. I call it perseverance.

What other things did your father teach you besides chess?

My father loved to teach me things. He taught me how to draw, fish, fly a kite, and ride a bike. He told me his stories about his poor background and how he came to the United States. He encouraged me to study harder, because the one thing he regretted in life was not being able to attend more schools when he was younger. Those were all the normal stuff.

He also taught me obscure things. He taught me about racism when I didn't even know what racism was. He taught me how to fix things around the house. He even taught me to stay at least one bathroom stall away from the next guy in a public bathroom.

Probably the most interesting thing that he taught me was how to think outside of the box and to be aware of people's ulterior motives. He did it by telling me a fable that he came up with when he was in prison for trying to escape from Communist China. The fable went like this:

In ancient China, there once lived a poor farmer with three sons. They all lived in a house that fitted only one family. One day, that farmer was diagnosed with a terminal illness. He decided that it was time to write his will before he passed away. He divided up his money and farmland evenly, but he did not want to divide up his house. He wanted just one of his sons to have it so that there wouldn't be any disputes later on when the sons get married and the house gets too crowded. The problem was that he didn't know which son to give the house to, and he did not have the luxury of time to find out. So, he decided to set up a week-long challenge to settle the manner once and for all.

He brought all of his children to his bedroom and told them about his dilemma. He then told them that he decided to give the house away to whoever was the first one to get him out of the house without physically moving him or physically hurting him in any way.

The eldest son said, "That's easy. I'll just set fire to the house, and then you'll be forced to leave the house." He then started to go look for a torch to set his father's bedroom on fire.

The father was disappointed with his eldest son's solution. "Please stop! If you set fire to the house, then there wouldn't even be a house left for you to inherit," he replied.

The second eldest son said, "I can make a lot of noise to annoy you so that you'll want to leave the house."

"I can always cover my ears to block out the noise," the father replied. "Plus, after being scolded by your mother's nagging voice every night, I've developed immunity to noise."

The eldest son then said, "I came up with a better solution. I'll take away all of the food in the house. And then, when you're starving, you'll be forced to leave the house to find food." He then went to the food pantry and threw out all of the food that was in there.

The father was slightly less disappointed with the response. "I like your solution, but I'm used to going on for days without food and water," he said. "So, is that the fastest way to get me out of the house? If so, then it looks like my eldest son will get the house."

The three sons looked at each other and didn't say anything. It looked as though nobody had a better solution. It looked like the eldest son was going to get the house.

The youngest son then spoke. "This challenge is too easy. Since you're confined to this house, we can all just keep taking away the things you need until you're forced to leave the house," he said. "I have a better challenge. Why not challenge us to force you to go back into the house?"

The father agreed that the challenge his youngest son proposed was a much more difficult challenge. Since he had access to all the things he needed in the outside world, it would be much more challenging for his sons to get him back into the house. He also didn't like the idea of starving for several days.

So, he brought all of his sons outside of the house. "Okay," he said.

But before he could propose his new challenge, his youngest son said, "I already won." His brothers looked at each other baffled.

"What do you mean you won? You didn't even get me back into the house yet," his father asked.

"That wasn't the challenge," the son said. "The challenge was to get you out of the house as soon as possible without physically forcing you to leave the house."

The father was stunned at the realization that he was now standing outside of his house just a few minutes after he had made his challenge. He decided to give his house to his youngest son.

After his father passed away, the youngest son sold the house and bought three smaller houses with the money. He then gave two of those houses away to his brothers.

"Pride, disappointment, and fear all go away when you don't expect to live another day. What's left is what's important. Our time on this Earth is short. Make it count, son."

– My Father

References

Chen, Bingan. *Big Fleeing.* Guangdong People's Publishing House, 2010. Print.

Chua, Amy. *Battle Hymn of the Tiger Mother.* New York: Penguin, 2011. Print.

Slumdog Millionaire. Dir. Danny Boyle. Prod. Christian Colson. By Simon Beaufoy. Perf. Dev Patel, Freida Pinto, Madhur Mittal, Anil Kapoor, and Irrfan Khan. Fox Searchlight Pictures, 2008.

Stanley, Thomas J., and William D. Danko. *The Millionaire next Door: The Surprising Secrets of America's Wealthy.* Atlanta, GA: Longstreet, 1996. Print.

Trademarks

AdSense, Android, and Google are registered trademarks of Google, Inc.

AIM and AOL are registered trademarks of AOL, Inc.
Amazon is a registered trademark of Amazon in the United States and other countries.

App Store, Apple, iPad, iPhone, iPod, and iTunes are registered trademarks of Apple, Inc.

Commodore is the trademark of Commodore Holdings, BV, registered in the United States and other countries.

Diablo, Starcraft, World of Warcraft are trademarks or registered trademarks of Blizzard Entertainment, Inc. in the U.S. and/or other countries.

EarthLink is a registered trademark of EarthLink, Inc.

Facebook is a registered trademark of Facebook, Inc.

GunBound is a registered trademark of SOFTNYX Co., Ltd.

Instagram is a registered trademark of Burbn, Inc.

Lamborghini logo, Lamborghini, Aventador, Gallardo are registered trademarks of Automobili Lamborghini Holding S.p.A.

NetZero is a registered trademark of NetZero, Inc.

Pandora is a registered trademark of Pandora Media, Inc.

Samsung is a registered trademark of Samsung in the United States or other countries

Secret Entourage is a registered trademark of Secret Consulting, LLC

Wii is a registered trademark of Nintendo.

Windows and Bing are registered trademarks of Microsoft Corporation in the United States and other countries.

TO BE CONTINUED...

Continue the story by following Allen Wong on Facebook:
http://fb.com/allenapp

If you like the book, please leave a review on Amazon.com:
http://amzn.to/lifehackedbook

MEET ALLEN

He's the developer behind many best-selling apps such as **5-0 Radio** and **Police Scanner+**. He became a self-made millionaire before he was **25**.

But, life wasn't always this grand for him. He was the only person in his family earning an income. And, he came from an oppressed family that grew up in the slums. Regardless, the apps he published were downloaded by over **25 million** people.

Now, he's sharing the story on how he did it, the crises he struggled with, and the advice his father gave him on how to be successful in both life and business.

Made in the USA
San Bernardino, CA
11 November 2015